SOMETHING TO WRITE HOME ABOUT

Also by Seth Swirsky

Baseball Letters

Every Pitcher Tells a Story

Baseball fans peer through the wooden slats of the outfield fence at the Polo Grounds, 1908

SOMETHING TO WRITE HOME ABOUT

GREAT BASEBALL MEMORIES
in Letters to a Fan

SETH SWIRSKY

Crown Publishers
New York

Published by Crown Publishers, New York, New York.
Member of the Crown Publishing Group, a division of Random House, Inc.
www.randomhouse.com

CROWN is a trademark and the Crown colophon is a registered trademark of Random House, Inc.

Printed in Singapore

Library of Congress Cataloging-in-Publication Data
Something to write home about; great baseball memories in letters to a fan / by Seth Swirsky.—1st ed.
  Includes bibliographical references.
  1. Baseball—Anecdotes. 2. Letters. I. Swirsky, Seth.
 GV873 .S66 2003
 796.357'02—dc21   2002031189

ISBN 0-609-60894-0

10 9 8 7 6 5 4 3 2 1

First Edition

Art Direction and Design by Seth Swirsky

For the two SUNS in my solar system, Julian and Luke

Contents

It all came together, the sunshine and the music, and I said to myself, "Man, how fortunate you are to be playing this beautiful game in this beautiful country!"

—Ernie Banks

Preface

Long before computers transformed the way we communicate with each other, the phrase "something to write home about" was universally understood to be an experience so unique and unforgettable that it could only be conveyed by a colorful, detailed, and often impassioned handwritten letter. Today, it is a vanishing phrase because letter writing itself is a vanishing phenomenon.

Yet, as you will read, the art of letter writing remains a valued form of communication for everyone from pinch hitters to presidents and from cultural icons to the common man. And all the letter-writers in this book share one very special thing in common: a memory that connects them to baseball.

I fantasize that well after my book's shelf life is complete, children of the future will scale the stairs of their grandparents' attics—as I did to reach my grandmother Mimi's musty, relic-laden treasure trove in New Haven—to dust off this book, and they'll agree that the stories they've read were, indeed, something to write home about.

Seth Swirsky

Los Angeles, California

November 2002

THE WHITE HOUSE
WASHINGTON
Mr. Seth Swirsky
WASHINGTON DC 200 SA
PM
1 MAY
2001
NBC NEWS
A Division of
Mail
First
Mr. Seth Swirsky
Seth Swirsky
33 USA

SOMETHING TO
WRITE HOME ABOUT

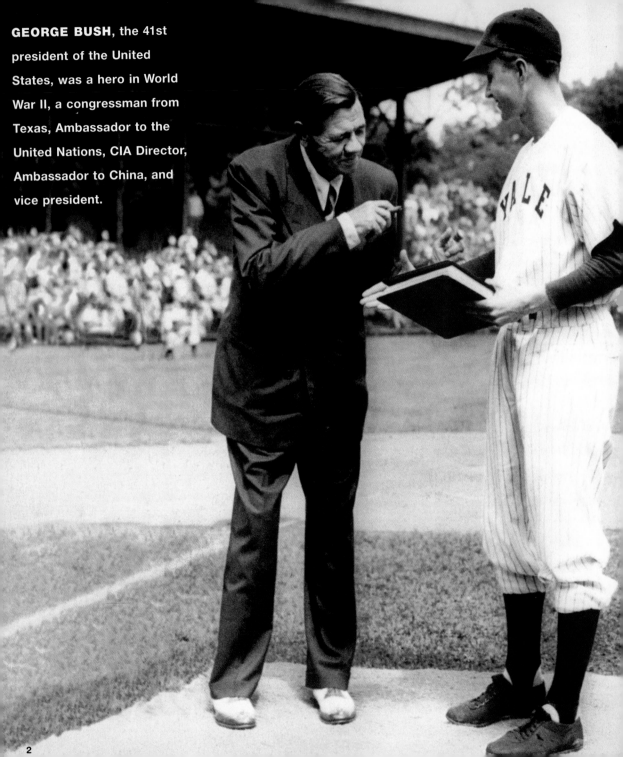

GEORGE BUSH, the 41st president of the United States, was a hero in World War II, a congressman from Texas, Ambassador to the United Nations, CIA Director, Ambassador to China, and vice president.

1-24-02

Dear Setter—

Baseball has always given me "something to write home about."

I'll never forget the spring of 1948 when Babe Ruth came to Yale Field. I was Captain of Yales team so I got to go on the field to receive some papers from the Babe. Riddled with throat cancer he could barely speak. But it was his very commanding presence that I'll never forget. Bent over, his body wasted, he was still the great Babe Ruth that every baseball loving kid in America wanted to emulate.

I had a lot of wonderful moments as Vice President and as President — great seats at great events; but the Babe at Yale topped them all —

G. Bush

10000 MEMORIAL DRIVE · HOUSTON, TEXAS 77024

Known as "Spikes" at Yale, the president kept his college mitt in his Oval Office desk drawer.

FLIP SCHULKE is an internationally acclaimed photojournalist, best known for his photographs of the U.S. civil rights movement in the 1960s, when he traveled extensively with Dr. Martin Luther King, Jr.

A Sunday Afternoon with Dr. Martin Luther King, Jr. And his Baseball Son, Marty.

Occasionally, when in Atlanta, on a Sunday, I would go to Ebenezer Baptist church, to hear Dr. King speak.

Afterwards he would invite me to his house for one of Coretta's great chicken feasts.

I never took photographs. We both would rather talk and he, play with the kids.

When I got out of my car that Sunday, he told me to bring my cameras, I asked "why"—And he replied, "It's not every day one learns that one has won the Nobel Peace Prize."

we had lunch in The dining Room, where
A Picture of GANdhi looked down on The
Family.

AFTER Lunch, The kids went To The
Back Yard To PLAY — As They USUALLY did
on A Sunday AFTERNOON.

Yoki in A Swing/glider where She Could
hAve close, PrivATe ConversATions with
her DAd.

Dexter Liked his DAd To Push
him on his Swing.

Bunny was So Young, ThAT her FAvoRiTe
PLAY WAS A Mild "Rough house" with
her dAd And EspeciALLy Liked Being
Tossed in The AiR — SqueeLing with pleasure
ALL The Time —

MARTY's FAVORITE WAS PLAYING BASEBALL
with his dad. They worked on The Basics
of CATCH And Throwing The BASEBALL.
BUT his FAVORITE FORM OF "PLAYING BALL"
WAS LEARNING how To "hiT". His DAD would
Pitch, under handed so ~~so~~ MARTY could
LEARN The "Swing" And how To hiT.

I had Seen This PLAYING BASEBALL MANY Times
AFTER Sunday dinners in The PAST — BuT This
SPECIAL Sunday I goT To Record The Love
And CARing exhibited By BoTh DR. King
And The 4 Children — A MORE hands-on
FATHER I had RARELY Seen in My work
AS A PhotoJournaList.

DR King WAS A GREAT FATHER, FAMiLY MAN And
A VERY good BASEBALL Coach —

Flip Schulke
MARch 28, 2002
West PalM BeAch, FL.

9

United States Senate

WASHINGTON, DC 20510–2101

December 12, 2001

Dear Seth:

Thank you for sending along the photograph of my brother Bob with Mickey Mantle. It was taken on Mickey Mantle Day in September of 1965. Bobby had recently been elected to the United States Senate from New York, so he stopped by the dugout that day to shake hands and extend his congratulations. That was when the photograph was taken. The picture that Mickey signed to him has been on my office wall for years. Bobby wanted to pay his respects to a magnificent player who was an icon in the world of baseball and a hero of the New York Yankees – but I like to think that his heart remained loyal to the Boston Red Sox!

One of the most memorable days we had together was when we both took my father to see the Red Sox play the Twins at Fenway Park in 1967. It was enormously exciting because the Red Sox won 6 to 4 and it was the game that clinched the pennant. Jose Santiago was the pitcher that day and he was kind enough to give me the winning ball. I have it on display in my Boston office, along with the MVP and Golden Glove Awards won that same year by the Red Sox's remarkable Carl Yastrzemski.

With all good wishes,

Sincerely,

Edward M. Kennedy

GATES BROWN was the most feared pinch hitter in baseball when he played for the Detroit Tigers from 1963 to 1975. His first hit in the majors was a pinch home run, and his clutch hits off the bench for the Tigers helped them win the 1968 World Series. I wondered what he considered his most memorable pinch hit.

Seth,

We were playing a day game in Detroit + Norm Cash, who wasn't playing that day, + I usually got hot dogs for each other every inning or so.

I knew Manager Mayo Smith didn't usually call on me until the 7th inning but this day he called on me in the 6th inning + as I said Norm + I were on the end of the bench eating them. I couldn't leave them there because I knew when I came back they wouldn't be there. So, I put the hot dogs in my Jersey + went up to hit.

Of all the times I didn't care if I got a hit would you believe I hit one up the gap + had to go head-first into second. When I got up, I had mustard + ketchup all over the front of my jersey.

When I got back to the bench, everyone was laughing like hell, all except Mayo who was livid. He fined me $100 + said the only reason he didn't fine me more was because I wasn't making too much money (smile)
end of story.
Gates Brown

13

JULIA RUTH STEVENS is one of Babe Ruth's two daughters. At 85, she remains a fan of her father's first team, the Boston Red Sox.

New Year's Eve, 1935. From left: Julia, Babe, Dorothy, and Babe's wife, Claire (seated).

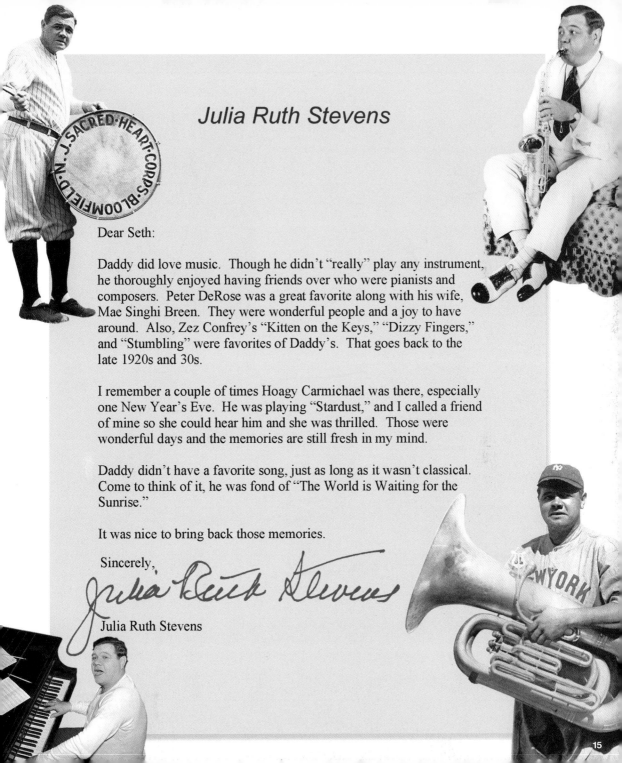

Julia Ruth Stevens

Dear Seth:

Daddy did love music. Though he didn't "really" play any instrument, he thoroughly enjoyed having friends over who were pianists and composers. Peter DeRose was a great favorite along with his wife, Mae Singhi Breen. They were wonderful people and a joy to have around. Also, Zez Confrey's "Kitten on the Keys," "Dizzy Fingers," and "Stumbling" were favorites of Daddy's. That goes back to the late 1920s and 30s.

I remember a couple of times Hoagy Carmichael was there, especially one New Year's Eve. He was playing "Stardust," and I called a friend of mine so she could hear him and she was thrilled. Those were wonderful days and the memories are still fresh in my mind.

Daddy didn't have a favorite song, just as long as it wasn't classical. Come to think of it, he was fond of "The World is Waiting for the Sunrise."

It was nice to bring back those memories.

Sincerely,

Julia Ruth Stevens

Julia Ruth Stevens

15

I saw **PAUL McCARTNEY** on TV at a Yankee play-off game in 2001 with his then-fiancée, Heather Mills. When the Beatles hit "I Saw Her Standing There" was played over the loudspeaker, he started dancing and singing to the delight of the crowd. I asked Sir Paul if he liked hearing his music in unexpected places and how he became a fan of American baseball.

_mpL

Dear Seth,

I became a Yankees fan when my friend Lorne Michaels got seats for us in 2000.

It was the first game Heather & I had actually been to! So we became instant fans.

Yeah, it was pretty cool hearing my music played at a game, ...it's just a pity that they didn't win this year, but, if they had to lose, it couldn't have been to a better state — Arizona!

Go Yankees,

Cheers!

Paul McCartney

P.S. My favorite Paul songs are "Penny Lane," "We Can Work It Out," "The Backseat of My Car," and "Junk."

SHAWN GREEN is the power-hitting right fielder for the Dodgers. His 49 home runs in 2001 were the most hit in the 117-year history of the franchise. I asked him to recount "the Rosh Hashanah [the Jewish New Year] story," and what went into his decision not to play on Yom Kippur (the holiest day of the Jewish year).

11/1/01

Dear Seth,

As a Jewish player in the Major Leagues, I've had numerous interesting experiences. I've had the pleasure of meeting fascinating people throughout North America who have reached out to me because I am Jewish. There are many Jewish, die hard baseball fans out there, yet there are few of us out there on the field. One night, however, back in 1996 in Milwaukee, I was not alone. At the time, I was playing for the Toronto Blue Jays. As I walked up to the plate and manicured the dirt in the batter's box before my first at bat, I greeted the catcher, Jesse Levis, and the umpire, Al Clark. This is something I always do my first time to the plate. I knew Jesse fairly well, and therefore I knew he was also Jewish. I greeted him, "What's up Yid!" and he replied "Not much Yid!" (this was an ongoing joke in reference to us both being Jewish). Meanwhile, strike one goes by me, and Al Clark looks at me and says, "By the way, Happy New Year." I stepped out of the box and said, "Al, you're Jewish?" Jesse replied, "Of course, you didn't know that?" We then proceeded to wish each other "happy new years" and I proceeded to strike out! This is one memory of baseball I will never forget.

Though I didn't grow up in a religious household, I was raised with a strong sense of identity. I was a huge baseball fan, just like lots of kids. At the time I was growing up, there really weren't any well-known Jewish players (at least as far as I knew). I was, however, very aware of Hank Greenberg and Sandy Koufax and the tremendous role models they were for Jewish people everywhere.

As my baseball career progressed, I always remembered the decisions that the two greatest Jewish ballplayers made, and I told myself that if I was ever in a position to, in any way, fill that role, I would. Thus, I feel a strong responsibility to make the right choices when it comes to such topics as not playing on Yom Kippur. I'm not trying to be "the next Greenberg or Koufax," but I am trying to do my part as a Jewish ballplayer.

Sincerely,

On May 23, 2002, Shawn had the greatest single day at the plate in the history of Major League Baseball, going 6 for 6, with four home runs, a double, and a single.

LEONARD GARCIA
was the batboy for
the California Angels
from 1965 to 1967.
I wondered how his
face ended up on
Aurelio Rodriguez's
1969 Topps baseball
card, making him
the only nonplayer
to appear on a
baseball card.

AURELIO
RODRIGUEZ
3rd Base

ANGELS

**Southwest
Professional
Baseball
School**

462 S. Gilbert Rd. Suite 599 • Mesa, AZ 85204

Dear Seth —

In 1967, we went on a season ending trip to Detroit. Aurilio had just been called up from El Paso. He was 19 and I was 18 at the time. During Batting Practice, I wore uniform #34 and Aurilio wore #37. We were playing catch when a photographer came up and took our picture. We told him he wrote our names down in the wrong order. He must have forgotten to correct the mistake before sending the photos to Topps.

I didn't know why coach Amaro kept calling me 'Aurilio' until one day in 1969, I was in the Angel clubhouse and saw the card. Everyone had a good laugh. Jim Fregosi knew of the mistake all along and thought we did it on purpose. He may have put the photographer up to it.

By the way — I now work for Topps!

A Brooklyn native, the actor **ELLIOTT GOULD** has appeared in more than 70 films since the late 1960s, including *Bob and Carol and Ted and Alice* (1969), for which he was nominated for an Academy Award, *M*A*S*H* (1970), *Nashville* (1975), and *Ocean's Eleven* (2001).

Dear Seth,

Our Fathers were invincible, All powerful, omnipotent. We depended on them so deeply, that it was inconceivable that they could be fallible or mortal. It was October 3, 1947. The Brooklyn Dodgers were facing the Yankees in game four of the World Series at Ebbet's Field. The unlikely Bums vs. the vaunted Bronx Bombers. My friend Donny Kramer lived across the street on West 9th. I had just turned 9. Donny's father Larry, suddenly and unexpectedly died that day. I asked my mom if I could invite Donny in to listen to the rest of the game with us. The Dodgers were losing 2 to 1. It was the bottom of the ninth, and Floyd Bevens, the Yankee pitcher, was unbelievably hurling a no hitter. There were two out.

Elliott and Donny, 1947.

Brooklyn had two runners on base, Gianfriddo on second and Miksis on first, when Burt Shotton, the Dodger manager put Cookie Lavagetto up to pinch hit for Eddie Stanky. On a one strike pitch, Lavagetto lined a double off the right field wall scoring Gianfriddo and Miksis giving the Dodgers a miraculous victory. It was a magical moment. It transcended the shock, the tragedy, and the loss of my friends father for a moment, a brief moment, but a moment none the less, reflecting spirit and hope in the darkest hour.

With love and devotion to all our fathers and mothers, Forever, I remain a fan.

Elliott Gould

Hall of Fame pitcher **TOM SEAVER** (311 wins, three Cy Young Awards) was the "Amazin' Mets" "go-to" guy in the hot-fun-in-the-summertime of 1969. Two games stand out: On July 9, against the first-place Cubs, Tom's perfect game was ruined, with one out in the ninth, when an obscure player named Jimmy Qualls (in just his 19th game) singled.

Two months to the day later, Tom beat the Cubs again to bring the Mets to within one game of first place. The night before, the writing was on the wall for the Cubs as a black cat ran in front of their dugout. They would never see first place again.

DAILY ☁ NEWS
NEW YORK'S PICTURE NEWSPAPER ®

MORE THAN TWICE THE CIRCULATION OF ANY OTHER PAPER IN AMERICA

104   New York, N.Y. 10017, Thursday, July 10, 1969

SEAVER PERFECT TILL 9ᵀ QUALLS GETS ONLY CUB HIT

NEWS photo by Ed Clarity

Jerry Grote rumbles home on Seaver's second-inning single. Randy Hundley awaits ball.

NEWS photo by Walter Kelleher

Met pitcher Tom Seav mows down Cubs 1-2 1-2-3, 1-2-3, etc. en rou to near-perfect night Shea Stadium. It was until the last inning th Cub Jimmy Qualls spo ed perfect game wi single to left. But Me won second game in r from Cubs, 4 - 0, a moved to within thr games of first place.

So? Who Perfect?

Cub manager Leo Dur cher sits glumly in th dugout but just abo all the 59,083 fans in th stands are on their fe to cheer as Seaver come to bat in the eighth i ning, when his perfec was still alive. He sacr ficed Al Weis to secor this time. "He'll prob bly never be that fa again as long as h lives," Leo volunteere after the game.

SETH —

WARMING UP IN THE BULLPEN — RUBE WALKER,
MY PITCHING COACH — KNEW I HAD EXCEP-
TIONAL STUFF THAT NIGHT VS. THE CUBS.
JIMMY QUALLS WAS THE ONE PLAYER IN
THE LINE UP I HAD NEVER FACED AND. I
KNEW NOTHING ABOUT HIM. HE IN FACT
HIT THE BALL HARD ALL THREE TIMES
HE CAME TO THE PLATE. I REMEMBER
TELLING MYSELF THAT IF ANYONE IS
GOING TO GET A HIT, IT WILL BE
QUALLS (NOT WITHSTANDING BILLY WILLIAMS),
BECAUSE I DID NOT KNOW HIS
STRENGTHS OR WEAKNESSES. I HAVE
NEVER SEEN QUALLS SINCE. AND I DO
RECALL THE BLACK CAT COMING ON THE
FIELD.
                    VERY BEST,

Seaver wore this jersey
during the Qualls game.

Before there were lights at Wrigley Field, there was **ERNIE BANKS**. He was one of the great hitters of his day (1953–1971), hitting 512 home runs and winning two MVP awards. I asked the Hall of Famer how he arrived at his signature phrase, "Let's Play Two," and what he experienced playing at Wrigley Field.

DR. ERNIE BANKS "MR. CUB"

December 17, 2001

Dear Seth,

The phrase "Lets's Play Two" came into my life naturally. I was driving down Lake Shore Drive in Chicago on a 110 degree summers day, in 1969, listening to music - Nat King Cole was singing '. . . bring out those hazy, lazy days of summer. . .' and I just felt the spirit of the game in me. At that moment, I felt the love of baseball. It all came together, the sunshine and the music and I said to myself "Man, how fortunate you are to be playing this beautiful game in this beautiful country!" I just looked at the whole picture of my life and thought about all the people around the world and other planets and how I'm just a little dot on this Earth but I got to play baseball. It was such a wonderful moment! The closer I got to Wrigley Field, the happier I became. I said to myself "Wow, such a beautiful, nice warm and perfect day for baseball, PERFECT!

I got to the ballpark, singing as I entered the clubhouse. Everyone was kind of walking around in slow motion it was so hot and I said: "GOD IT'S A BEAUTIFUL DAY - LET'S PLAY TWO!!!" and everybody kind of woke up. Billy Williams and Ron Santo said "You're always crazy - what are you talking about playing TWO today? Get out of this clubhouse!" But I said "just look at this beautiful day, we should play two!" A writer, Jimmy Enright, picked up on it and still, everywhere I go that's what I hear: Ernie Let's Play Two! The phrase reflects how much I truly, truly love baseball.

There were two elements of playing in Wrigley Field. You had baseball in the afternoon and love at night. I played in the Sun and Moon: I had love at both ends - During the day I was playing the game I loved and I had love at night being with my wife and family, who loved me. Most players today don't get a chance to play in the sunlight. Just playing baseball under the sun, in nature, that's beauty.

I used to love hitting home runs at Wrigley. When I was fortunate enough to hit a home run, I said in my mind before the pitcher released the ball: "Now it's time for me to take a little ride" and I imagined myself being inside of that ball as it went out of the park.

My Very Best To You

Ernie Banks

60 EAST CHESTNUT STREET, SUITE 412 • CHICAGO, ILLINOIS • 60611-2012

ELIZABETH WRIGLEY-FIELD

is a college student living in New York.

Dear Seth,

I've always loved having a name people get a kick out of! My mom's last name is Wrigley and my dad's is Field, but they didn't think they could give a kid the last name Wrigley-Field — that would just be too weird, and the kid would probably be teased.

I thought that was ludicrous. I'm not a baseball fan, but I've always loved how excited my name makes people. Plus, the Cubs fans I've met have been a spirited bunch. They seemed like a good group to get associated with because they all seemed to genuinely adore the stadium with my name. So in first grade, my desire to be noticed for a funny name everyone liked combined with my feminist sensibilities (it seemed fairer to have both my parents' names than just my dad's) made me start referring to myself as Elizabeth Wrigley-Field and everyone's called me that since.

I guess people really like my name because it's unique. I'm an only child, and Wrigley and Field (as opposed to Fields) are both uncommon names, so I assume I'm the only person in the world with my last name. Still, I'm holding out for one day meeting an Alex Fenway-Park or something similar. We'll have so many stories to swap!

Sincerely,

Elizabeth Wrigley-Field

GAYLORD PERRY won 314 games and two Cy Young Awards during his Hall of Fame career (1962–1983). Pitchers are not expected to be home-run hitters and Gaylord was no exception. It took him seven years to hit his first one, strangely fulfilling the visionary prediction of his first manager, Alvin Dark.

Seth,

a writer for the S.F. Examiner paper told Alvin Dark that this Kid - Gaylord Perry - will Hit some Home runs for you. Alvin said, a man will land on the Moon before Gaylord Perry Hits a Home run.

The day they landed on the Moon, I was pitching — about 30 minutes later, I Hit my first Home run !

Gaylord

BUZZ ALDRIN was the second man to set foot on the moon — on July 20, 1969. That very day, the #1 song in the U.S. was the futuristic "In the Year 2525," by Zager and Evans. Buzz's destiny may have been preordained, as his mother's maiden name was Moon.

Buzz Aldrin
Astronaut

Seth —

I've thrown a few first pitches.... for a minor league team in Iowa, and for the Anaheim Angels in 1999. It sure felt good — but if I were pitching on the MOON — it would have floated a lot farther!!

Buzz Aldrin

34

asked **RON SWOBODA**, a key member of the
69 New York Mets, if he had been aware of the
gnificant times he was living in when he played
e game. (Pictured right: Ron's spectacular
orld Series catch in game four of the '69 Series.)

Dear Seth,

1969 was an incredible year without the Mets winning a World Series. The War the protests, the social upheaval, the recent assassinations of King and Kennedy, mixed in with the Moon landing and unprecedented good economic times. It seemed like all things were possible and all things were happening simultaneously.

We were young people in a liberal New York and I took my leanings from that. But with the focus you need to play major league baseball I was more insulated from the tumult though certainly not unaware!

P.S. YOU ASK TOO LARGE A QUESTION HERE!

Sincerely,
Ron Swoboda
1969 METS

PETER TORK was a member of the pop group The Monkees (from left: Davy Jo[nes],
Michael Nesmith, Mickey Dolenz, and Peter). Their zany Saturday morning TV show, c[]
with their huge hit singles ("I'm a Believer," "Daydream Believer," "Last Train to Clarks[]
among others), catapulted them to superstar status from 1966 through 1968.

Nov. 27, '01

Dear Seth,

After the Monkee phenomenon died down,
I knocked around for a while, eventually
getting a couple of teaching jobs in the L.A.
area through my then wife, who was then an
educator herself. One of these two teaching
jobs was also to be the baseball coach, at a
small prep school in Beverly Hills, an opportunity
I jumped at!

It was fascinating and harrowing. I was not
yet sober at the time, and while not actually
under the influence while at school, I was not,
sadly, at my best most of the time, either.

But! It remains a high point of my life.
I get a huge charge out of telling anybody
interested that I was a high school baseball
coach, and some of the individual memories rank
very high on my top whatever number list.

For instance — The 1st day, I was standing

behind third base when the batter lost the bat which came whirligigging at me, full-tilt. I thought: is this a test? Talking batting, pitching, fielding and so on... To be immersed in that role, and to participate — at ANY level — with the game as it's actually played will stay with me — and very fondly — to the end of my mental life.

One other note — you might think that having a celebrity for a baseball coach would jazz the kids, but I saw very little of that. They called me "coach," as was proper, altho' I might have preferred the more egalitarian "Peter." But, our interactions were all about the game. You know, celebrity disappears very shortly when you're actually there.

Peter Tork

Many people have fond memories of playing Wiffle ball in their backyards.
DAVID J. MULLANY is the grandson of the inventor of the game.

THE **WIFFLE BALL** INC.
275 BRIDGEPORT AVENUE
P. O. BOX 193
SHELTON, CONN. 06484-0193

November 9, 2001

Dear Seth —

My grandfather, David N. Mullany was born & raised in Hatfield, MA on a tobacco farm.

On his way home from job hunting one day, he noticed my father and his friends playing a game in the backyard with a plastic golf ball and broom handle. It was a highly competitive game needing few players and a limited amount of space.

He and my dad, David A. Mullany, set out to create a plastic ball that would curve controllably with little effort and wouldn't damage property. After several tries, they ended up with a design for the ball we manufacture today with 8 oblong holes on one half.

They named the ball and the game they played "WIFFLE." (In dad's neighborhood a swing and a miss was a "wiff" and the new ball produced lots of them!)

As to your question regarding WIFFLE and life in general .... I think it's simplicity is still appealing. We find ourselves barraged with rules & regulations on a daily basis. We're required to obtain licenses and authorization to conduct just about any activity. Now, I'm not saying that going out and playing WIFFLE will solve all (or any) of that but how many games are left where kids, or adults, are the captains of their own ship? How often do you make the rules? A ball hit off the chimney is a home run? OK! It's an out? Fine by me! How many strikes to an out? 1? 2? 7? You decide. It's your backyard. Play any way you want!

Best regards,

David J. Mullany, V.P.

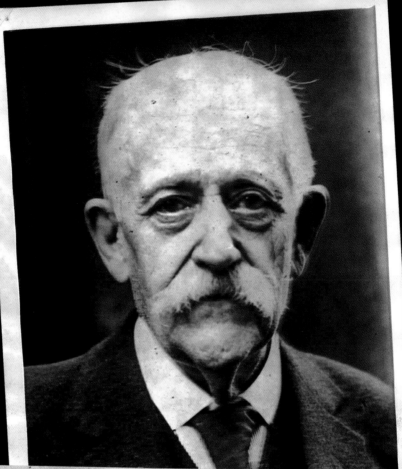

This photograph of **CORNELIUS SAVAGE** appeared in the *International Tribune* newspaper on August 11, 1921.

154081   International

HE PLAYED BASEBALL WHILE LINCOLN WATCHED.

This is Mr. Cornelius Savage, who has the distinction
of having played baseball in the backyard of the White
House, with President Lincoln as a spectator. Mr.
Savage was born in New York, and he remembers many details of the life of the great President.

On one occasion President Lincoln intervened in
behalf of several boys who were ordered to stop playing
ball on the White House grounds, by the Public Building
Officer.   The gentleman above happened to be one
of the boys.   B-11-21

The front and back of the White House (during Lincoln's tenure, 1861–1865), where Cornelius and his friends played baseball. In those days, children cut through the grounds on their way to and from school. The sculpture (top) is of Thomas Jefferson, and it stood from 1841–1875.

4001 Nebraska Avenue, N.W.
Washington, DC 20016
202 885-4548

A Division of
National Broadcasting
Company, Inc.

Timothy J. Russert
Moderator
Meet the Press

Since 1991,
TIM RUSSERT
has been the hard-hitting, fair-minded moderator of "Meet the Press," the longest-running show in television history (1951 to present). He is also the Washington Bureau Chief for "NBC Nightly News with Tom Brokaw."

June 5, 2001

Dear Seth,

I grew up in BUFFALO, N.Y. My favorite birthday present was to pile into our 1955 green Chevy station wagon and drive 4 hours to Cleveland for an Indians vs Yankees doubleheader. It was the only major league baseball game I saw all year so I begged to stay to the last out.

I _now_ realize how hard 18 innings and eight hours of drivin was on my Dad and my Uncles.

while they had to stay alert on the way home, I slept leaning against the ice chest in the back of the wagon.

My favorite player was Yankee catcher, Number 8, Yogi Berra. My dream was to get his autograph or catch his foul ball. Never did. Sitting in the upper level was not conducive to either!

Fast forward 40 years. My son Luke and I are invited to the White House on March 30, 2001 to meet the Hall of Famers.

Within moments I'm talking to Yogi Berra. Then Whitey Ford too. The greatest pitcher - catcher duo of my boyhood.

Eight weeks later, I interviewed Yogi. It was one of the most interesting, fun, and in a remarkable way emotional hours of my life. My life with my Dad — and now with my own son — inextricably linked to baseball — and Yogi Berra. Father and son forever. And yes — I got Yogi's autograph. So did Luke. And we got one for my Dad too.

Tim Russert

P.S. Luke thanked President Bush for inviting him to the White House and showing him the Oual Office. He seemed to suggest he might have a chance for the Hall of Fame <u>And</u> The Presidency! Very funny — but I will never get in the way of a 15 year old's dreams. After all I met Yogi Berra — in the white House.

3. 17. 01

Dear Seth,

The season is close, and I am ready for opening day. I will be throwing out the first pitch this year (probably a cut fast ball) in Milwaukee. What an honor to do so as the President.

I love baseball. My affection must have had its start when I watched the '48 Yale Bulldogs practice and play the game. My Dad was on first; Mother, the scorekeeper.

Top: Two future presidents, 1948.
Bottom: "43" and "41" in '02.
Right: In a (little) league of his own, 1954.

It grew in West Texas as a little leaguer (catcher for the Cubs) and as a tossing Companion with #41 (President G. H. W. Bush). I still remember catching his left-handed throws.

I remember my hero, Willie Mays, my first game in the Astrodome (Morgan hit a homer), and being introduced as a General Partner of the Texas Rangers.

I treasure my memories of the great game and look forward to collecting a lot more of them starting soon. Best regards,

RICHIE SCHEINBLUM played for eight seasons in the major leagues, starting out with the Cleveland Indians in 1965. His best year was with the 1972 Kansas City Royals, where he hit .300 and was selected to the American League all-star team.

June 10, 2002

Dear Seth,

This is to relate my entry story into baseball. In 1964, many of the major teams who had scouted me over the preceding years invited me for tryouts at their home ballparks. My father, my college coach and friend, Dom Anile, from world famous C.W. Post College, and myself set up an itinerary and set off for our first location, Pittsburgh, PA. We traveled by train in those days, in lieu of stagecoach, to save time.

I had a great workout at Forbes Field in Pittsburgh and proceeded to go to my personal locker, located in the boiler room adjacent to the visiting L.A. Dodger locker room. I had never met a major league player before, so when Frank Howard and Tommy Davis from the Dodgers came into the boiler room to wish me well, my confidence was boosted for the walk up to the offices of Pittsburgh General Manager Joey Brown, Jr. He told me they would like to sign me for $8000, and while I was still trying to catch my breath, I heard my college coach say we would think about it.

I was revived from my coma during our train trip to Cleveland and never did ask Coach Anile why there was any reason to think about an offer of $8000. My father, on the other hand, being a CPA in New York, already had figured out City, State, and Federal tax on $8000, plus expenses incurred on this trip, as deductions.

I hit the ball well at my tryout with Cleveland and again made the trip up to the General Manager's office and met an excellent ex-player, Hoot Evers. As he was sitting at his desk talking about baseball, he pulled out his glove that he used when he played in the seventeenth century and very casually mentioned, "The Cleveland Indians would like to offer you..." to which I jumped up, almost across his desk, and shouted:

"I'LL TAKE IT!"

The offer was for $12,000, luckily. My dad and I went out into the hall to talk, and I said to him, "Dad, we're getting $12,000. You and I never have to work another day in our lives." He agreed, and we trained it home.

In fond retrospect of my father's joy that day,

Richie Scheinblum

Richie Scheinblum

Being the 1st Black coach in the M.L. was bitter sweet for me. Sweet because I was with the Big League team, but bitter because I knew men who were capable to coach & manage in the M.L. seventy five years ago.

Buck O'Neil

In 1962, **BUCK O'NEIL** was named the first African-American coach in major league history by the Chicago Cubs. I asked the former Negro Leaguer how he felt about his unprecedented appointment.

Ernie Banks congratulates Buck.

1997 marked the 50th anniversary of Jackie Robinson's historic breaking of the color barrier in baseball. To honor him, Baseball Commissioner Bud Selig required every major league team to retire #42, Robinson's number. When slugger **MO VAUGHN** (325 home runs and counting, and 1995 A.L. MVP) became a New York Met in 2002, he asked if he could "borrow" the number.

To Seth,

I think it's a tremendous honor to wear #42 in N.Y.C. I have always stated that this is not my number, I just wear it to keep a legacy alive.

Jackie Robinson was the man that changed this country and its history forever.

His struggle gave all minorities an opportunity to shine in every sports venue. Every man, woman and child can benifit from his story!

I would hope to be half the man Jackie Robinson was and all he represented. That would be a successful and productive life!

Everyone remembers where they were when the United States was attacked by terrorists on Tuesday, September 11, 2001. I asked the ninth commissioner of baseball, **BUD SELIG**, how he learned of the attacks and if he was stung by the criticism of some prominent major leaguers who thought the rest of the season should be canceled.

Office of the Commissioner
MAJOR LEAGUE BASEBALL

ALLAN H. (BUD) SELIG
Commissioner of Baseball

October 25, 2001

Dear Seth:

Thank you for your letter of October 19, 2001.

In answer to the questions you have raised, I was home when I heard about the attacks. It was a stunning moment. We were to have an Owners Meeting in Milwaukee that day so I was getting ready to conduct a full Major League Meeting which, of course, I called off.

I was clearly not affected by Mark McGwire's criticism and, in fact, most people were extremely complimentary of how the situation was handled. It turns out that the following Monday was absolutely the right time to re-start the game. However, I did talk to a lot of people in Washington and New York to gauge their opinions and then finally made the judgement that I came to. Fortunately it all worked out well.

I have often said Baseball is a social institution with social responsibilities and I hope that in some small way Baseball has played a role in the healing process. I hope, as the head of this social institution, the voice of the Commissioner of Baseball contributed to some stability after the horrific events of September 11th.

I hope this has been helpful.

Sincerely,

Allan H. Selig
Commissioner of Baseball

AHS:sar

777 E. Wisconsin Avenue
Suite 3060
Milwaukee, WI 53202

ED RENDELL has been district attorney and mayor of Philadelphia. A former chairman of the Democratic National Committee, he is currently the Democratic nominee in the 2002 governor's race in Pennsylvania.

EDWARD G. RENDELL

Dear Seth:

As Mayor of Philadelphia from 1992-2000, I had the opportunity to meet and work with many heroes - police and firefighters who risked their lives every day, teachers who worked for low pay because they were dedicated to improving children's lives and ordinary moms and dads who struggle to make a better future for their children.

Of the many heroes I met, however, one embodies this spirit. His name is Michael Springer, a Vietnam veteran, who was walking down the street when he saw a baby perched on the third floor window ledge of a neighborhood rowhouse. Realizing the baby was in danger, Mr. Springer planted himself on the sidewalk below. Just seconds later, the baby fell out of the window, but Mr. Springer caught it and saved it. He truly made the "Catch of a Lifetime." We celebrated Mr. Springer's heroism in City Hall. Rawlings Sporting Goods makes and presents the annual "Gold Glove" awards to Baseball players for being the best fielders at their position. They awarded him a Gold Glove for his "great catch", the only time they gave one to a non-player. It was a great day for our city - to honor a great everyday hero like Michael Springer.

Sincerely yours, Ed Rendell

57

On August 20, 1938, Cleveland Indians catcher Frank Pytlack caught a ball that was thrown 708 feet off the Terminal Tower in Cleveland by his teammate Ken Keltner. It is the highest structure from which a baseball has ever been caught.

Longtime Indians pitcher, 93-year-old **MEL HARDER** (223 wins from 1928–47), is the last living witness to that event.

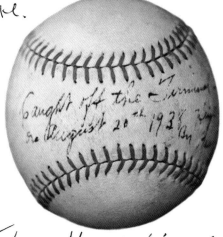

Dear Sett:

It was difficult to pick-up the ball from that Height. Frank Pytlack missed a couple but then finally he caught one.

Then, the Indians 2nd string catcher Hank Helf caught one. So we were proud that two of our catcher were able to catch a ball thrown off the Terminal Tower. It was difficult to do.

Regards

Mel Harder

Seth,

A little backround - my Dad and I were with the Dodger organization at the same time - but Never at the same level. When I was in the minor league, he was Vice Pres. in charge of Scouting. When I was in the major leagues he was Vice Pres. in charge of Both Scouting + Minor leagues UNTIL Dec 13th 1968. I think it was a Friday.

Mr. OMalley Named My DAD General manager in charge of player personnel — 15 min. later I was Traded to K.C. Royals for $150,000 and two players. He told me that if he was Named G.M. it would be a hard Decision to make -- He waited 15 min. to trade me. IN his Defense - I got a Big Raise to play for K.C. Also the Dodgers had two Young catchers in Double and Triple A Named Joe Ferguson and Steve Yeager.

But I think I'm Still the ONLY player that was Traded By his DAD

Jim Campanis

P.S My DAD DieD ON Fathers DAY.

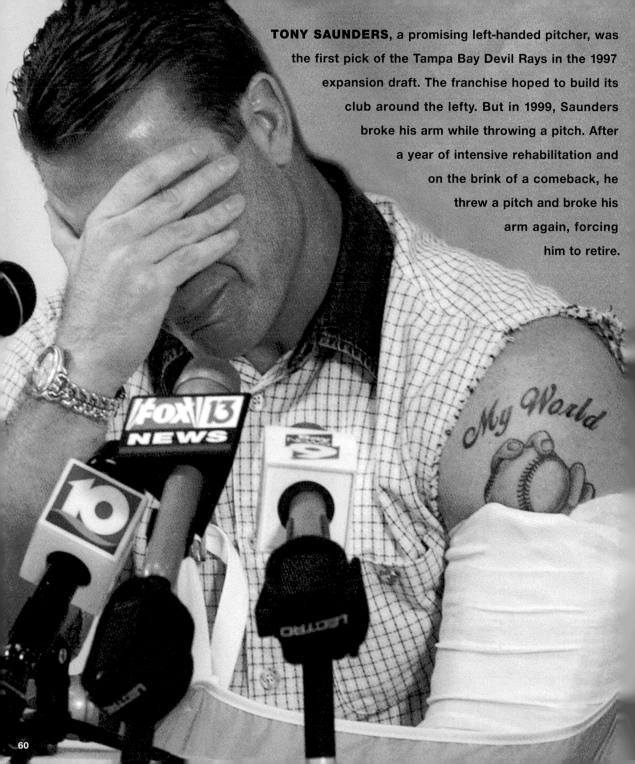

TONY SAUNDERS, a promising left-handed pitcher, was the first pick of the Tampa Bay Devil Rays in the 1997 expansion draft. The franchise hoped to build its club around the lefty. But in 1999, Saunders broke his arm while throwing a pitch. After a year of intensive rehabilitation and on the brink of a comeback, he threw a pitch and broke his arm again, forcing him to retire.

Seth,

So many thoughts race thru my mind as
I know that I have to walk away from a game that I
love so much. The hardest part of the whole thing is
letting go of something that I have worked so hard to get.
There are also other thoughts that enter my mind. What am
I going to do for the rest of my life, hell I'm only 26 years
old? Do I write out a formal retirement letter or do I just
speak from the heart? Those are tough questions for me to
have to answer right now, but they have to be done and answered.
I guess I will just speak from the heart as I did
Everytime I stepped out on the mound and went to battle for
my Teammates. I feel as if there is a huge chunk of my
heart missing with nothing to fill it. I have dedicated my
whole life to a dream and now it is time to let it go. But
it is also another opportunity and a new beginning for whatever
it may be...

#31

Tampa Bay Devil Rays
Tropicana Field • One Tropicana Drive • St. Petersburg, FL 33705 • 727-825-3137 • 727-825-3245 Fax • www.devilrays.com

61

Dear Seth,

Here's how I recall the scene late in Game 6 of the '86 World Series: When the Red Sox got 2 in the top of the 10th, NBC dispatched me to their clubhouse for the post game. As the Mets came up in their half, plastic was already covering the Red Sox lockers, champagne was at the ready, the championship trophy was wheeled in on a special cloth-covered stand, and next came the very frail Mrs. Jean Yawkey, well into her eighties escorted by Commissioner Ueberroth, anticipating the first Bosox title since she was a girl.

Bob Costas

I stood on a platform constructed for the post game with a monitor in front of me and an earpiece providing me with Vin Scully's play by play.

I was thinking not only of the specific questions I might ask about this series, and this season, but what might be appropriate to say concerning this first Red Sox World Series triumph in 68 years.

Then Carter singled with two out. Mitchell followed with a hit. I asked Mike Weisman, our executive producer, "What do I do if the Mets tie it?" "If that happens, get the hell out as fast as you can!"

After knight's fisted single and the wild pitch to Wilson, The game was tied. You could feel Shea Stadium rocking. Mrs. Yawkey, head down, saying nothing, was gently escorted away. I took out the earpiece.

Technicians began dismantling the set-up. Clubhouse men ripped the plastic off the lockers, all accomplished as quickly as a set change at a Broadway show.

By the time Wilson's grounder got by Buckner, the last camera had been rolled out into the corridor.

I was the last to leave, coming ~~out the~~ out the
clubhouse door just as the first of the
Red Sox traipsed down the tunnel from
the dugout. Many appeared ashen-faced;
but maybe that was my imagination.

This much I know for sure—There was
total silence until someone, I'm
not sure who, smashed a bat
against the wall of the tunnel and
bellowed a single expletive. There
was silence again after that.

That scene remains as dramatic
and vivid, and human, as any scenes of triumph
I've ever witnessed.

Bob Costas

COMMONWEALTH WINERY
Boston Red Sox
1986 Champions
Cranberry Blush

CARBONATED CRANBERRY APPLE WINE
PRODUCED & BOTTLED BY
COMMONWEALTH WINERY
PLYMOUTH MASSACHUSETTS   BW-MA 2   ALC. 9% BY VOL.

William Hayward **"MOOKIE" WILSON**—his family gave him his nickname because of the funny way he said "milk" as a child—fouled off six of nine pitches in his heroic at bat before hitting that "little roller up along first" that won game six of the 1986 World Series.

Pictured below is the ball that went through Bill Buckner's legs—"the Mooki ball." It was picked up in right field by umpire Ed Montague, who gave it to Mets traveling secretary, Arthur Richman. Richman handed it to Mookie in the jubilant Mets clubhouse. After Mookie signed it, the ball was passed around and kissed by all the players.

NEW YORK NATIONAL LEAGUE BASEBALL CLUB

Dear Seth,

There were a few lessons to be learned from the 86 World Series. Always Hustle and give your Best. Some say it was luck that Bill Buckner missed that ball I hit, but I believe you make your own luck, because if I had not been running hard down the Firstbase line, things might have turned out different. In other words, My Hustle caused the error.

So remember, Never give up and always Hustle and give it your Best, Not only in sports but in everything you do because great things happen when you do.

Mookie Wilson

Harry Frazee (1880–1929) was a larger-than-life character in the worlds of theater and baseball during the 1910s and '20s. His 65 musical productions—the most famous being *No! No! Nanette!*—earned him wealth and prominence. (In June 1927, he hosted the welcome-home gathering for aviator Charles A. Lindbergh upon his return to the United States after his historic flight to Paris.)

In 1916, Harry bought the World Champion Boston Red Sox for less than $400,000. (The team was sold in 2001 for an estimated $700 million.) Although the Sox had won the Series again in 1918—their fourth championship of the decade—by 1919 Harry was selling many of his best players including Babe Ruth to the Yankees in order to keep the team financially solvent. Poor attendance to Red Sox games made it impossible for him to pay his players. When Ruth was sold, in fact, very few Boston rooters were upset (Ruth's career hadn't yet taken off).

Before Ruth's departure, the Red Sox had won 15 pennants and six World Series. After he was sold to the Yankees, they lost the Series four times (1946, '67, '75, and '86, all in the seventh game), while the Yankees, who pre-Ruth had never won a Series, went on to win 26 titles in 38 appearances. Many fans believe that the divergence of the two teams' fortunes is directly related to Harry's sale of the Babe, referring to it as the "curse of the Bambino."

MAX FRAZEE is Harry's great-grandson. His letter attests to the still-strong feelings elicited by the sale of Babe Ruth 73 years earlier.

SETH,

THERE WAS NO "CURSE OF THE BAMBINO". IT WAS JUST A GOOD BUSINESS DECISION AS WELL AS A MYTH PORTRAYED IN THE PRESS TO KEEP THE FANS BELIEVING IT WAS "BIG HARRY'S" FAULT RATHER THAN THE BOSTON TEAM.

IN 1993, I RECEIVED A CALL FROM THE BOSTON RED SOX TO COME TO FENWAY PARK TO RECEIVE A WORLD SERIES PIN, WHICH WAS NEVER GIVEN TO THE CLUB AND ITS MEMBERS FOR THE 1918 WORLD SERIES VICTORY. WHEN I ARRIVED, THE RED SOX TREATED ME VERY WELL. WE HAD A FEW LAUGHS, THOUGH IT WAS A BIT IRONIC, GIVING A PIN TO THE MOST HATED MAN IN THE HISTORY OF THE BOSTON RED SOX.

THE SOX WERE PLAYING KANSAS CITY THAT DAY AND THE CEREMONY WOULD BE BEFORE THE GAME. ALL THE PARTIES WERE LINED UP ON THE 1ST BASE LINE NEAR THE BOSTON DUGOUT TO RECEIVE THE PIN. WHEN THEY STARTED TO PASS THE PINS TO THE INDIVIDUALS BEFORE ME, THE FANS APPLAUDED. WHEN THEY GOT TO ME I WAS RECEIVED BY 35,000 BOOING FANS. IN MANY WAYS THIS _is_ WHAT I EXPECTED. AFTER ALL THE BOO'S SETTLED DOWN, I WAS SMILING AND SAYING TO MYSELF, "IF ONLY THE FANS REALLY KNEW THE TRUTH ABOUT BIG HARRY, I DOUBT THEY WOULD HAVE BOOED."

MAX FRAZEE

PAUL GIORGIO is a real estate investor living in Massachusetts. When the Red Sox next win the World Series, they might just have him to thank.

Dear Seth,

I attempted to Reverse the "Curse of the Bambino" by taking it to New heights. I climbed Mount Everest in 2000 and met a Tibetion Holy Man called a "Lama". After I came home in the fall of 2000 and saw the New York Yankees win yet another World Series title, I turned to my wife and said that I'm going to visit "The Lama" in 2001 and see if there's anything I can do to "Reverse the Curse".

So on my 2001 Everest Expedition I visited with the lama and he advised me to get the Boston Red Sox cap blessed at base camp ceremony called a "Pujan". After that ceremony I needed to place the cap on the Summit of Everest.

After those 2 procedures took place I was to burn a New York Yankees cap in the pujan fireplace as an "Offering to the Gods". Well I completed the cycle to break the curse and can only hope the Boston Red Sox win the World Series.

Sincerely Yours,

Paul George

BABE RUTH's parents sent him to reform school when he was seven years old, deeming him "incorrigible." Baseball turned out to be his savior, and the rest is history. In this letter to his agent's son, written shortly after his retirement from the game, the Babe offers his sage advice.

October 26, 1935.

Dear Christy:-

Your Daddy has just told me that you are
now a student at St. John's Military Academy.

When I was a young boy I attended St.
Marys School at Baltimore, where the good
Brothers were very patient with me and helped
me a lot toward future life. I am sure the
Sisters at St. John's will help you.

But the main thing in life to remember
is that your success and happiness in the
future will depend upon your own efforts and
not the money or clothes which you might receive from your parents. The most successful
men that I know today were poor boys.

Wishing you success and happiness, I
am,

Yours,

Babe Ruth

Master Christy Walsh, Jr.,
St. John's Military Academy,
Los Angeles, California

73

Bob is in the back row, second from left. His roommate is in the front row, far right.

Dear Mom & Pop   July 26, 1949

Say Dad you aught to be down here it is really delightfully cool. They say they are having the funniest weather they ever had here in Kansas. But it has really been nice and cool.

I room with Mantle, the shortstop. He was hitting .230 a week and a half ago, he went on a hitting streak and jumped up to .300 in that time. He is fast as lightning, hits and bunts. I'll close for now.

                        Love
P.S.   Bob
The mosquitoes chew you to death down here, I never saw so many

Untold numbers of players have said that one of their biggest thrills is hearing their names announced over the Yankee Stadium public-address system. The man who has announced those names since April 17, 1951 (the day of Mickey Mantle's first game), has been **BOB SHEPPARD**. At 91, his distinctive voice still echoes through "the house that Ruth built."

The last time I saw Mickey Mantle was a few months before his death.

I introduced him on "Good morning, America."

He told the interviewer that he got "goose pimples" every time I announced his name.

So did I!

Players don't correct me when I pronounce their names. That's because I go to <u>them</u> and ask how their names should be pronounced.

That's my job!

You asked for a poem.

Here's one I wrote 15 minutes after ROGER hit 61:

"<u>ROGER MARIS SAYS HIS PRAYERS</u>"

They've been pitching me low,
They've been pitching me tight.
I've grown so nervous, tense and pallid.

But my prayers are full of joy to-night —

Thank you, Lord, for Tracy Stallard.

Bob Sheppard

eddie layton

AT THE MIGHTY WURLITZER

HIGH F *Custom*

MERCURY MG20433 · EDDIE

EDDIE LAYTON has been the organist for the New York Yankees since 1967, one of three left in baseball. He has recorded 26 albums of his own music.

ddie is credited with reating the original rgan music to the mous stadium hant, "CHARGE!"

New York Yankees

Dear Seth:

During the week, I am in the recording studios making TV and radio commercials. a limo takes me to Yankee Stadium around 4 or 5 PM. at that time, I have my dinner in the Press room. After the game, the limo takes me home.

I love baseball but I hate rain delays and extra innings.

When the Yankees are away, I spend time on my boat which is docked in Tarrytown on the Hudson river.

I am looking forward to another 35 years of playing the organ here — then I'm getting out of the bisness. all the best,

Eddie Layton

JOEY LAURICE (1927–2002) was the brother of Shorty Laurice, the man who started the Dodgers Sym-phony in 1938. The Sym-phony, along with "Howling" Hilda Chester and her cowbell, Eddie Bettan with his tin whistle and explorer helmet, and Jack Pierce with his helium balloons, were part of the festive atmosphere at Ebbets Field until the team left for Los Angeles after the '57 season. I asked Joey how the band first formed.

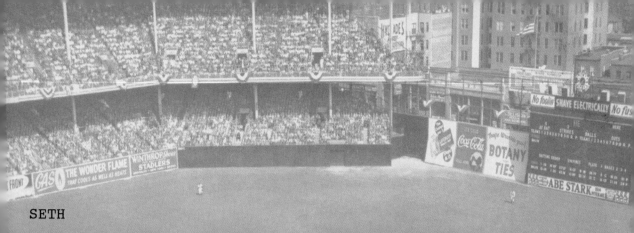

SETH

THERE WAS NO 'IDEA' TO START THE DODGER SYM-PHONY.
MY BROTHER, CARMINE JACK (SHORTY) LAURICE HAD BEEN GOING TO
EBBETS FOR YEARS AND SAT IN SECTION EIGHT FIRST ROW SEAT ONE.
A FEW FELLOWS, BROTHER LOU SORAINO, PADDY PALMER, JERRY MARTIN,
PHIL, JOJO, MYSELF... ALL THE BOYS... WERE OUR BAND.

WE WOULD GO AROUND THE STANDS AS THE GAME STARTED. THE
FANS LOVED IT. ORGANIST GLADYS GOODING WOULD STOP PLAYING. WHEN
THE VISITING TEAM CAME TO BAT AND STRIKE OUT, THE BAND WOULD
PLAY 'WORMS CRAWL IN' AND WHEN THE PITCHER WAS TAKEN OUT,
SHORTY AND THE BAND WOULD PLAY 'HOW DRY I AM' (WITH LITTLE
JOJO ON THE BIG BASE DRUM) AND THE FANS,THEY WOULD LAUGH.
I COULD GO ON AND ON.

SHORTY AND THE BAND GOT FREE ADMISSION AND ROAD TRIPS BY
THE CLUB. THEY WERE GIVEN THE NAME DODGER SYM-PHONY BY RED
BARBER. WHEN SHORTY PASSED AWAY, HE WAS GIVEN A DAY AT THE
BALL PARK. SEVERAL FANS SENT FLOWERS. JACKIE ROBINSON AND
ROY CAMPANELLA, BRANCH RICKEY, WALTER O'MALLEY CAME TO
SHORTY'S FURNEAL. HE IS BURIED RIGHT NEAR GIL HODGES.

THE LAST STOP THE HURSE STOPED IN FRONT OF WAS EBBETS FIELD...

Joseph S Laurice

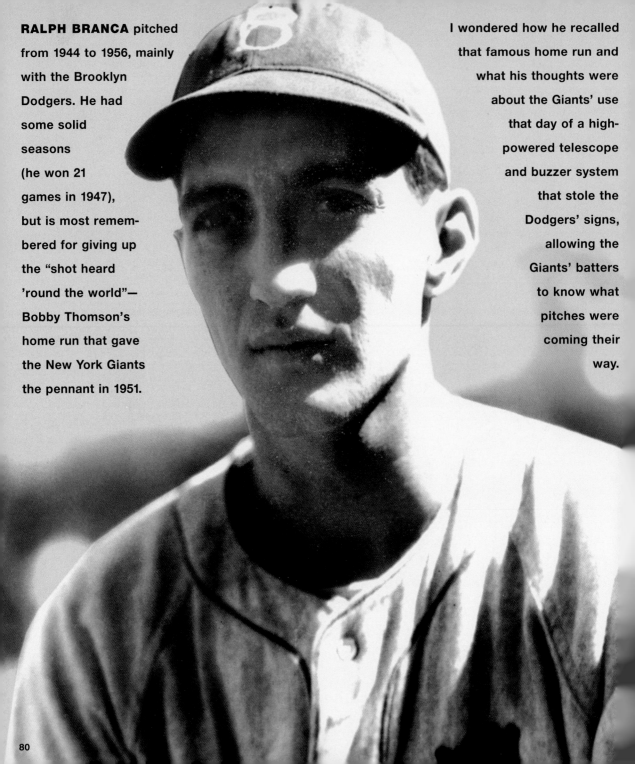

RALPH BRANCA pitched from 1944 to 1956, mainly with the Brooklyn Dodgers. He had some solid seasons (he won 21 games in 1947), but is most remembered for giving up the "shot heard 'round the world"— Bobby Thomson's home run that gave the New York Giants the pennant in 1951.

I wondered how he recalled that famous home run and what his thoughts were about the Giants' use that day of a high-powered telescope and buzzer system that stole the Dodgers' signs, allowing the Giants' batters to know what pitches were coming their way.

Dear Seth,

There are things I remember about Oct. 3, 1951 and others "we simply choose to forget."

Before the game I remember kidding with Pee Wee Reese and Jackie Robinson about having "butterflies." An expression used by ballplayers to denote nervousness.

I was designated to be the first pitcher out of the bullpen, even though I had pitched eight innings two days earlier on Monday, Oct. 1st. My arm was very stiff, so I started to throw in the sixth inning to be sure I would have enough time to get loose. Actually, I lob-tossed from forty to forty-five just to get loose.

My arm eventually loosened up so I was able to throw very well and in reality I believe at full strength.

I don't remember the walk in from the bullpen, but I do remember meeting Pee Wee and Jackie on the infield grass and asking "Anyone got butterflies?"

The first pitch I threw was dead center and Thomson took it for a strike. The next pitch was up and in, about chin high, and Bobby jumped on it. He hit it with an uppercut swing which promotes overspin. I remember saying or praying "sink - sink." Of course, it did sink, but not enough and cleared the wall.

That made baseball history!!

In 1954, when I first learned how the Giants had stolen the signs from the sanctity of their lockerroom and used an electronic device to transmit the signs, I was astonished!! I also was incensed because I consider it the most despicable act in the history of the game, but on the other side of the coin I was relieved that I now knew what I had always known in my heart, that we were a better baseball team on the field and with much more moral integrity.

Best regards,

Ralph Branca

For the record, Branca has said: "Even if [Thomson] knew [a fastball] was coming, you can't always hit it. At home-run-hitting contests, they know what's coming and they'll pop it up."

The "shot heard 'round the world" game was the first to be televised coast to coast. This photograph shows fans watching it in San Francisco (where the New York Giants would move to in 1958).

At the game that day were FBI Chief J. Edgar Hoover, Frank Sinatra, and several New York Yankees (waiting to see who their World Series opponent would be). With the Dodgers taking a commanding 4–1 lead into the bottom of the ninth inning, Yankee catcher Yogi Berra, known for his phrase, "It ain't over till it's over," left the ballpark. But the game wasn't over. **BOBBY THOMSON** remembers.

Hi—

Going into last half of 9th inning losing 4 to 1, I felt totally depressed. I didn't think I would get a chance to hit, being the 5th hitter, with Newcombe looking so strong in the eighth.

As it turned out, the score became 4 to 2 when I got up to bat. Don Mueller injuring his ankle sliding into third stopped the game for me — broke the tension — got my mind away from the game.

Wasn't until Mueller was carried off the field, my mind returned to the game. Walking to home plate, I was in my own world thinking about what I had to do: get back to fundamentals.

Wait for the ball - don't get over anxious - do a good job -- give yourself a chance to hit. I called myself an S.O.B. all the way to home plate. I had never done anything like that before in my life.

Arriving at home plate, I realized for the first time, the Dodgers had changed pitchers - I felt no pressure, just went through the motions, in my own little world, getting ready to hit.

I hit an inside fast ball for the homer and experienced excitement I hadn't felt before.

Sincerely,
Bobby Thomson

Thomson (left) celebrates the Giants' victory with winning pitcher Larry Jansen and Sal "the Barber" Maglie.

Thomson's home run sounded differently depending on which team you were rooting for.

Dodgers radio announcer Red Barber:

"Branca pumps . . . delivers . . . the curve. Swung on and belted deep into left field. It is . . . a home run. And the New York Giants win the National League pennant and the Polo Grounds goes wild. [59 seconds of silence] Well, friends, we have to try to get back above the screaming, howling, tempestuous noise that has reached an unprecedented height. And never was there a more dramatic finish to a pennant race. There just couldn't be. There never was . . . such a playoff. And . . . the Giants coming to bat apparently a beaten ball club, 4–1, in the last half of the ninth inning have now ripped in four runs for the game, the playoff, the pennant . . . "

Giants radio announcer Russ Hodges:

"Hartung down the line at third, not taking any chances. Lockman without too big of a lead at second but he'll be running like the wind if Thomson hits one. Branca throws . . . There's a long drive! It's gonna be, I believe . . . ! THE GIANTS WIN THE PENNANT! THE GIANTS WIN THE PENNANT! THE GIANTS WIN THE PENNANT! THE GIANTS WIN THE PENNANT! Bobby Thomson hits into the lower deck of the left field stands. The Giants win the pennant, and they're going crazy, they're going crazy! Oh, ho!"

Dear Seth: April 22, 2002

You asked how I came to record Russ Hodges description of the Bobby Thomson home run — The Shot Heard Round the World.

I was 26 years old and working in an office in Manhattan. I knew I wouldn't have access to a radio but I wanted to hear the end of the playoff game. I was a long time GIANT fan so I set the RADIO to WMCA, set up my reel to reel tape recorder, showed my MOTHER what button to push when the NINTH inning started. I then took the BMT train to work.

That evening, I couldn't wait to get home to listen to the tape. I knew what had happened but I had to hear it for myself.

I rewound the tape and there was Russ Hodges Screaming "THE GIANTS WIN the pennant... I don't believe it... the whole place is going crazy."

The next day I wrote to Russ suggesting that if his STATION didn't record his "call" I could let him borrow my tape.

A few days later I got a call from Russ asking for the tape. I lent it to him. He used it to produce Christmas Cards that year and returned the tape with a note of thanks.

The years have passed but everytime that home run is shown on TV – with the soundtrack based on my tape – I smile and think to myself: "We did that – Ralph Branca, Bobby Thomson, Russ Hodges, me and MY MOTHER!"

Larry

Russ Hodges's microphone.

After playing for eight years in the minors, catcher **PAUL LO DUCA** was called up by the L.A. Dodgers in 1998. He rewarded them by hitting .320 with 25 home runs in 2001 and making people forget about a guy named Piazza.

A Brooklyn native, Paul honors his late mother by writing her name on his cleats before each game. Here, he is pictured as a member of the minor league Bakersfield Dodgers.

LOS ANGELES

Dodgers ®

1000 ELYSIAN PARK AVE.
LOS ANGELES, CA 90012-1199

Dear Seth,

My mother was such a big influence in my life. She taught me everything from patience and kindness to hardwork and determination. She was by my side and had a hand in all my accomplishments. From the soccer field, she would roam the sidelines to the baseball field, she cheered from the right field line. From the time she would take off work to sharpen my Batting skills. Sometimes it was off to the Batting cages but most of the time it took place right in our own Back yard. With sunglasses to shield her eyes she threw me pinto bean after pinto bean 'til my hands bled. I can still feel her presence today. I can still hear her say "Keep your head down" on every bad swing. She will always be with me for as long as I live. The only thing I regret is that my mother never got to see me play at the Big League level. But one thing is for certain Luci LoDuca and the Lord above both bleed "DODGER BLUE".

Paul LoDuca

BARRY WILLIAMS played Greg Brady (sixth from left) in the popular TV series *The Brady Bunch,* which aired on Friday nights at 8 o'clock on ABC from 1969 through 1974.

Dear Seth,

Growing up in Los Angeles, I was naturally a Dodger fan. I recall how classes were stopped in my elementary school so we could gather in the auditorium to watch the historic 1963 World Series, which featured two amazing pitchers for the Dodgers - Don Drysdale and Sandy Koufax. As a little league pitcher (and a right-hander) it was easy for me to relate to Drysdale. It was inspiring to watch as he dominated the batters, ultimately leading them on to victory in that series.

Nothing in my years was to prepare me for the day when "The Big D" actually walked on to our "Brady Bunch" set. In addition to the anticipation of meeting him, the story line revolved around his teaching my character to play baseball and how to pitch.

Don Drysdale (1936–1993) won 209 games while pitching for the L.A. Dodgers from 1956 to 1969. A fierce competitor, the crowning achievement in his Hall of Fame career was his record 58⅔ consecutive scoreless innings in 1968, since exceeded by Orel Hershiser in 1988.

At 6'5" 220 pounds, he was someone to be reckoned with. I recall the rumors of his pitching days and his intimidating philosophy - "hit one of mine, I hit two of yours." I didn't know what to expect of the "real" person.

The man I met was open, friendly, commanding and helpful. He was on our set for two days and proved to be at ease in front of the camera as well. What impressed me most was what went on between the takes. He didn't retire to his dressing room or disappear from the sound stage. Instead he hung around with my Bradymates and me to... play catch. That was better than having a role on a series!

In life there are a few special, unforgettable experiences that are shaped by coming into contact with someone you truly admire. For me, the two days Don Drysdale came to our set to teach "Greg" how to pitch is one of them.

Kindly yours,

Barry Williams

BARRY ZITO of the Oakland Athletics is one of baseball's elite pitchers, as well as a free-spirited, guitar-strumming Californian. I asked him to compare his favorite hobby with his profession.

January 2, 2002

Dear Seth,

I think of pitching a lot when I surf. There is so much downtime when you are out waiting for the waves that I often think about how I am going to approach hitters during the year. You would think that I would not think about the season that much now, in the off-season, but the truth is that it is always on my mind.

The two rushes you get in surfing and in baseball are definitely different. The rush of pitching is very controlled. You cannot let it get out of hand or else the game may get out of hand. So, in a sense, you can't really get all excited, and even if you do and show it, you look cocky and unprofessional. I would say the rush of surfing is a more free feeling. You can hoot and holler when you get a good ride, and be liberated to yell and get very excited.

Sincerely,

Barry Zito

BARRY BREMEN, a mer-
chandising executive living
in Michigan, is known as
"the Impostor," his stunts
the stuff of legend. In 1985,
he mounted the stage in
Pasadena, California, to
accept Betty Thomas's Emmy
Award for Best Actress for
her performance in *Hill
Street Blues.* (She wasn't
amused.) In 1979, Barry
high-kicked with the Dallas
Cowboys Cheerleaders. (The
Cowboys made him sign an
agreement never to appear
in a cheerleader uniform
anywhere near a Cowboys
game again.) When asked
by the *New York Times* what
compelled him to try to pull
off his stunts, he said, "It's
fun, but the biggest thing is
that you meet people."

I asked Barry what he
remembered about trying to
sneak into the 1979 All-Star
Game dressed as a New
York Yankee.

Seth,

I had just finished infield and outfield practice and all I was concerned about were the correct words to the National Anthem. It was Tommy John who helped me into the stadium and, the locker room. For a moment I was a New York Yankee! I will never forget how nervous I was.

When I joined the NBA All Stars, I wasn't sure what to expect. Would I be cought? Would I go to jail? What would happen? I was so nervous at first that I missed the basket all together and when I went for the rebound from George Gervin, well it had so much spin on it that I bobbled that also. I guess just nerves. My knees were weak and I was very light headed from all this excitement. The sounds of 60,000 fans were great! I had so much fun.

The moment I would never forget was when Otis Birdsong (who was a Kasas City King) and myself were talking on the sidelines and I had my Kansas City King uniform from four years before and he looked at me and said "You and I are on the same team and I don't even know who you is."

My best to you always

Barry Bremen

"The Impostor"

GENE MAUCH was a highly respected manager from 1960 through 1987, but he never won a pennant. Two of his teams folded under bitter circumstances: His 1964 Philadelphia Phillies were leading the St. Louis Cardinals by six games with nine to play and lost the pennant on the last day of the season, and his 1986 California Angels were but a strike away from their first World Series appearance in the ninth inning of game five, when Boston's Dave Henderson hit a home run to tie the game, which the Red Sox won. The Sox then took the next two games to steal the pennant. I asked Gene which disappointment was harder to take.

A toothache hurts on either side of the mouth.

Gene Mauch

CHARLESTON

RIVERDOGS

11·27·2001

Dear Seth,

How do I view Disco Demolition 22 summers later? Through the years, people have said it was a disgrace; some said it was a tragedy. Some said I had it coming; my Dad, Bill Veeck said "sometimes they work too well." What did I learn? I never mistake a lousy promotion with a tragedy. Besides, I didn't have enough talent to be in "Rolling Stone" any other way.

Fondly,
Mike Veeck

Field of bad dreams: Disco Demolition Night.

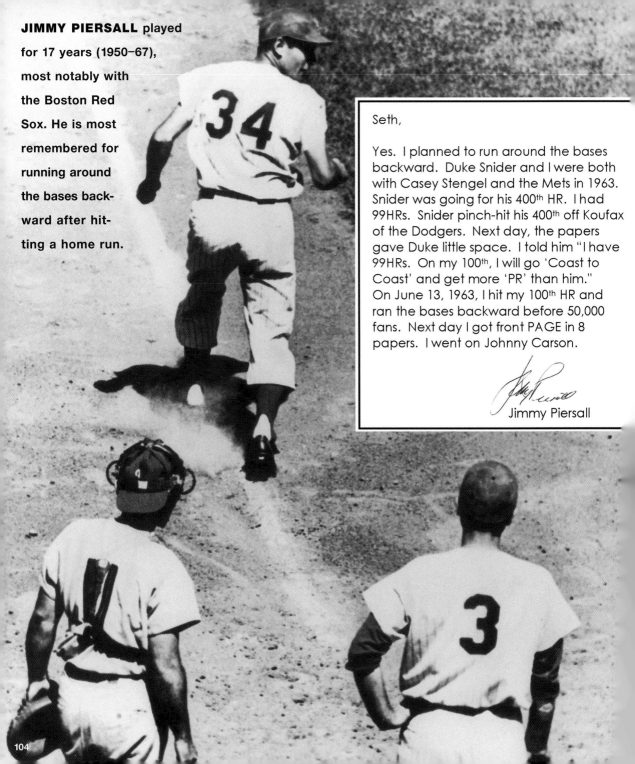

JIMMY PIERSALL played for 17 years (1950–67), most notably with the Boston Red Sox. He is most remembered for running around the bases backward after hitting a home run.

Seth,

Yes. I planned to run around the bases backward. Duke Snider and I were both with Casey Stengel and the Mets in 1963. Snider was going for his 400th HR. I had 99HRs. Snider pinch-hit his 400th off Koufax of the Dodgers. Next day, the papers gave Duke little space. I told him "I have 99HRs. On my 100th, I will go 'Coast to Coast' and get more 'PR' than him." On June 13, 1963, I hit my 100th HR and ran the bases backward before 50,000 fans. Next day I got front PAGE in 8 papers. I went on Johnny Carson.

Jimmy Piersall

WILLIAM S. COHEN was the U.S. Secretary of Defense from 1997 to 2001. A former congressman (1973–1979) and senator (1979–1997) from Maine, he is also a published author of nine works of fiction, nonfiction, and poetry. It is interesting to note how the man in charge of the world's most powerful military understood the necessity of restraint.

May 30, 2002

Dear Seth —

I played Little League at the tender age of 12. Except I was not very little. I stood 5'7" and weighed 125, considerably larger than most of my peers. I had a rocket arm with Nolan Ryan speed from the mound, which stood just 44 feet from home plate. However, I had all the control of an unguided Scud missile, and serious injury was a very plausible outcome for those brave enough to step into the box.

This fear created by my lack of control was my greatest weapon. I earned the honor of pitching the first No-hitter in Maine Little League history. I also struck out 18 batters in one game while walking 16!

Given my control problems, very few batters dug their rubber spikes in & got close in the box. But opposing coaches used this against me. They would send tiny eight-year-olds to the plate who could barely hold the bat. Standing in a crouch, looking more bewildered than afraid, they were little more than two feet from head to toe. I was paralyzed with fear of hurting them and practically had to roll the ball to the plate. What I gave up in speed I did not gain in control. The Lilliputians humbled the Bangor Brobdingnagian* as they walked to and around the bases with depressing regularity.

Through high school and college, I continued my pursuits on the mound, relishing the mano-a-mano challenge. I threw sliders, curve balls + knuckles

*The Lilliputians and the Brobdingnagians were the little and big people (respectively) in Jonathan Swift's classic, *Gulliver's Travels.*

As off-speed pitches with great gusto, but with no greater control.

It was only after I entered politics that I learned to throw the perfect pitch — straight down the middle . . . .

Bill Clinton

TINKER TO EVERS TO CHANCE is the most famous double play combination in the game's history, not owing to their defensive dominance as much as to a poem written in 1910 by a columnist with the *New York Evening Mail.* Shortstop Joe Tinker, second baseman Johnny Evers, and first baseman Frank Chance made their first double play for the Chicago Cubs in front of 200 fans on September 13, 1902. Because of a misunderstanding over taxi fare in 1905, Tinker and Evers didn't speak to each other until they were reunited at a Cubs World Series game in 1938, where they embraced and wept.

Joe Tinker

Frank Chance

Johnny Evers

Baseball's Sad Lexicon

These are the saddest of possible words:
"Tinker to Evers to Chance."
Trio of bear cubs, and fleeter than birds,
Tinker and Evers and Chance.

Ruthlessly pricking our gonfalon bubble,
Making a Giant hit into a double—
Words that are heavy with nothing but trouble
"Tinker to Evers to Chance."

—Franklin Adams, 1910

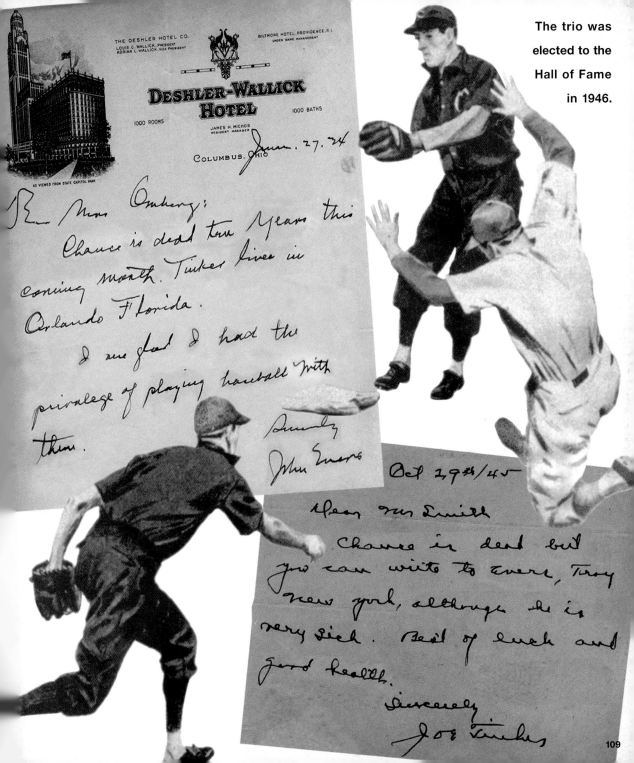

The trio was elected to the Hall of Fame in 1946.

THE DESHLER HOTEL CO.
LOUIS C. WALLICK, PRESIDENT
ADRIAN L. WALLICK, VICE PRESIDENT

BILTMORE HOTEL, PROVIDENCE, R.I.
UNDER SAME MANAGEMENT

DESHLER-WALLICK HOTEL

1000 ROOMS   1000 BATHS

JAMES H. MICHOS
RESIDENT MANAGER

COLUMBUS, OHIO June. 27. 24

Dear Miss Amberg;

Chance is dead two years this coming month. Tinker lives in Orlando Florida.

I am glad I had the privalege of playing baseball with them.

Sincerely
John Evers

Oct 29th/45

Dear Mrs Smith

Chance is dead but you can write to Evers, Troy new york, although he is very sick. Best of luck and good health.

Sincerely
Joe Tinker

109

RONALD REAGAN, the 40th president of the United States, portrayed Hall of Fame pitcher Grover Cleveland Alexander in the movie *The Winning Team* (1952). Old Pete, as Alexander was known, was one of the great pitchers of all time, winning 373 games (from 1911 to 1930) while struggling to conceal a then-taboo malady.

Ronald Reagan
with Frank Lovejoy
in *The Winning Team.*

Oct. 1

Dear Friend—

Having met "Old Pete" you should be interested in knowing about, "the best kept secret in sports," which we hinted at in the picture. The "fainting spells" in our movie were as close to the truth as we felt we should go. In addition to all his other troubles or probably under lying all his troubles was the terrible affliction of "Epilepsy". He tried to keep this secret all his life and we felt we'd tell the story without using the word.

Best

Ronald Reagan

Grover Cleveland Alexander (right) was named after the 22nd and 24th president of the United States, Grover Cleveland (1885–1889, 1893–1897).

As "the voice of the Washington Senators" from 1947 through 1961, Hall of Fame broadcaster **BOB WOLFF** (elected in 1995) had a unique perspective about the relationship that many U.S. presidents had with the "national pastime."

April 16, 2000

Dear Seth,

Opening Day in Washington was my best chance all season to shout at game's end, "The Senators are in first place!"

Not that the team lacked in talent — they lacked in numbers and in finances. They just couldn't afford enough stars at any one time.

It was exciting, competitive major league baseball though, and I was privileged to have a voice in it. When I arrived at Griffith Stadium for each new opener there was always hope — and there was preparation which included making a chart of who was in the presidential party and where each was sitting.

When Harry Truman was President,
the big topic was whether he'd make
his ceremonial pitch lefty or righty.
The ambidextrous Chief Executive would
not make this vital decision until
the last moment.

President Eisenhower was passionate about golf, but a baseball fan too. Occasionally, unannounced, he left the White House early, along with his entourage, to watch a game. In 1956, with Ike in attendance, Jim Lemon put on a show with three home runs in one game. I always had the theory that if presidents had come out more often, the Senators would have won the pennant.

President Nixon knew the game
and its players. One day, as Vice
President, I interviewed him on
radio as a "Fan in the Stands,"
and told him not to reveal his
identity until the climactic moment.
After seven minutes of baseball chatter,
I inquired:

"And what do you do in Washington?"
"I work for the government."
"Well, that's just fine. We have
    so many government workers here.
    What's your job?"
"I'm the Vice-President of the
    United States!"

Good straight men are tough to find.

With best wishes, Seth, Bob Wolff

115

Dear Seth:

When I was a kid playing baseball, my Dad said that when a coach/manager ever asked if I could play a position, I should say "sure". I never dreamed that it would ever happen.

When Johnny Oates asked if I wanted to do it that day I of course said "sure, let's go for it". I felt most nervous though when I took the mound to face the only hitter of my professional career. I had to take a deep breath a couple of times and, incredibly, struck out the batter on a 67 mph change-up.

What a joy it was to be able to do this on a day when, without Johnny Oates's knowledge, my family, including my father, happened to be there in person to share this moment with me.

God Bless,

The first to do it was Oakland A's shortstop Bert Campaneris (upper right) in 1965, followed by Minnesota Twins second baseman Cesar Tovar (right) in 1968, and most recently by Detroit Tigers shortstop Shane Halter (upper left) in October 2000.

Seth,

The subject you have asked me about is the incident with Tony Conigliaro. I will try to tell you how badly I felt about it.

It was an afternoon game in Boston. What a lot of people don't understand is that I had 2 outs and was ahead 3-1 in the 6th inning. The pitcher was the next hitter with nobody on base. I would have been foolish to throw at a hitter or even think about it.

I was a hard thrower and as soon as I hit him I knew it was bad. He went down right away. I felt very bad about it. I can still remember their dugout all up and yelling at me.

I tried to go to the hospital but only the family was allowed that night after the game. We had to leave town the next day.

It was the last time I ever played against him. If I could have seen him I would have apologized. I felt just awful. I was just a young kid trying to be a big league ballplayer and it was truly an accident.

The next time the Angels went to Boston to play I had to stay in a different hotel than the rest of the team because I had received threats against my life.

I am reminded about it every day (by someone) because I have a restaurant in a tourist area. I have even had people tell me or my family that they don't like me or even hate me because of an accident that happened over 30 years ago. But I can tell you or anybody who asks, from the bottom of my heart, I had no intention of throwing at him at all. I honestly know I could never throw a baseball at anybody's head.

Thanks for getting hold of me.

Jack Hamilton

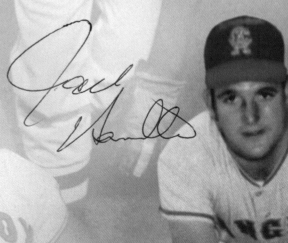

TIM SALMON, since entering the league in 1992, has hit more home runs (269 and counting) and driven in more runs than anyone who has ever put on an Angels uniform since the team was founded in 1961.

The Salmon family. From left: Callie, Jacob, Tim, Ryan, Marci, and Katelyn.

Dear Seth,

Being a Major League dad offers many challenges and rewards. The season requires us to be on the road half the time. Mom ends up playing the role of dad much of the time. When the kids are young they seem to change a lot between road trips. I've missed out on a lot of "first time events". Some of the rewards are when the kids watch me on T.V. and being home most of the time during the off-season. My children are still young so I'm not sure if they can truly appreciate what I do. Their friends are my teamates' children and their dads are on T.V. also. So I'm not sure being on T.V. is a big deal. My hope is that I can play long enough so that when the kids are older they can come into the clubhouse and field and really enjoy it for what its suppose to be... A dream come true! Sincerely, Jim

Infielder
WAYNE CAUSEY
(riding the second mule
from right) was a member
of eccentric owner Charlie
Finley's Kansas City Athletics
from 1961 through 1966. Finley's
promotional stunts ranged from Hot
Pants Night (with free tickets given
to women who wore them to a game) to
Harvey the Mechanical Rabbit (who popped
out of the ground to present the umpire with
new baseballs) to having a shepherd and grazing
sheep behind the right field wall. One of Finley's
more memorable gimmicks was having his team's
starting lineup enter the stadium riding a mule train.

Dear Seth,

The night Mr. Finley had the players ride the mules into the stadium — "Farmer's Night" — was only one of several mule events we had that year.

I most remember the mule event when the owner of the White Sox would not allow Mr. Finley to bring our team mascot, "Charlie O" The mule, into Comisky Park. Because of this, Finley hired several delivery men to deliver a large carton to our dressing room during the game. When they opened the carton, inside, there was a donkey. They pushed & pulled the donkey through the tunnel, to the dugout & onto the field. The umpire told our manager to get the mule off the field or he would eject every player from the game. The mule was quite stubborn & the game was delayed for several minutes.

Wayne Causey

JACKIE BRANDT was a member of the 1961 American League All-Star team. After he got a pinch hit, he came out of the game and took a shower. Wanting to see the rest of the contest, he toweled off in the runway near the dugout, unaware that he was in full view of a national television audience.

Actually Seth,
I did have some
shorts on. Most
people watching on
TV usually get
to see everyone
in uniform. I
guess this was
my chance to
show them what
a player looked
like at home,

Jackie Brandt

FRANK THOMAS was one of the game's top home run hitters during his 16-year career (1951–1966). As a member of the 1962 New York Mets, he found many ways to help his team, aside from his team-leading 34 home runs.

April 14, 2001

Dear Seth:

Players like to eat and eat fast so on chartered flights, as soon as we were high enough, I would help the stewardesses serve the players. I served the players and manager first and the trainer got mad because I didn't serve him right away. He complained but it didn't do any good. He got over it.

I served on every road trip the whole season and the players liked it because they got their food a lot faster.

By the way, I always ate last.

Sincerely,

Frank Thomas
The Original One

SAMUEL GOLDWYN
7210 SANTA MONICA BLVD.
LOS ANGELES

January 29, 1942

Mr. James Starr
Los Angeles Herald and Express
1243 Trenton Street
Los Angeles, California

Dear Mr. Starr:

On February second I will start shooting "The Pride of the Yankees," starring Gary Cooper as Lou Gehrig.

I have never produced a picture which has received so much public interest in advance or invited so many letters of suggestion and comment.

There are, however, several misapprehensions which have gained circulation with regard to the picture and which I feel it may be well to set right.

First of all, "The Pride of the Yankees" is not to be, in a strict sense, a "baseball picture." There are several factors, important though they may be, which have never been major considerations in the making of this picture. I have not been motivated, for example, by the fact that baseball is America's greatest sport, that no ambitious motion picture has ever been made with big league baseball as its background, or that 1941 was "baseball's greatest year."

The one thing that moved me to make this picture was the story of Lou Gehrig, the man. It is one of the most inspiring and, at the same time, tragic stories I have ever known. It is true. It is life. It is the highly dramatic and truly American success story of the son of a janitor and a fraternity house cook, both German immigrants. Lou Gehrig washed dishes to pay his way through college. He was not a "born ball-player" bu

struggled toward mastery in a sport for which originally he had no particular aptitude. His story is the story of this struggle, of his first romance and the girl he married. It is a story in which life itself is the villian, giving Lou Gehrig everything a man could hope for, and then snatching it away.

There has never in the history of sport been as moving a chapter as the events leading up to the July fourth in 1939 when Lou Gehrig, faltering in step and speech, stood up to a microphone in the Yankee Stadium and, with tears streaming down his face, said to the 60,000 people who had come to cheer him for the last time, "I feel today that I am the luckiest man on the face of the earth."

Baseball is simply the backdrop for this story which is, in a broad sense, the story of the opportunities that America offers every boy and of the whims with which life sometimes favors a few and then destroys them.

I feel that it would be something less than keeping faith with the thousands of baseball fans who idolized Lou Gehrig and the millions of others who admired this man to make "The Pride of the Yankees" anything less than the finest possible tribute that can be created to his memory. It is with this purpose that we enter upon production of the picture.

I hope you will be able to see much of this picture made and that we will have the pleasure of your visiting the studio often while it is in production. You are always welcome.

Sincerely,

Samuel Goldwyn

This press statement was issued by Joe DiMaggio upon the release of *The Pride of the Yankees*.

"Just as my locker in the Yankee clubhouse adjoined Lou Gehrig's, so his deeds and memory and above all his ideals as a man, will be close to my heart in the years to come."

"In the thick of another pennant race his former teammates take time out to congratulate Samuel Goldwyn on giving Lou's life to future generations through the medium of a motion picture."

"The Yankees are out to win the pennant this year and we sincerely hope that Lou Gehrig's picture will win the highest Academy awards."

Joe Di Maggio
(Signature)

The very stoic DiMaggio said he cried only twice on the field: on the day he was honored at Yankee Stadium in 1949 and when Lou Gehrig told the world that he was the "luckiest man alive" on July 4, 1939.

Seth—
My biggest moment in my career
was my 1st big league game.
My 1st base hit was a home run.
in my 1st game.
Watching Duke Snider, Pee Wee
Reese and all those Dodger
players in the same field
with me was like a dream.
The only thing that was
missing was my father.
He died three years before
I play my 1st game in the
big League.

Orlando Cepeda
Hof 99

THE AMAZING KRESKIN is the world's foremost mentalist or "mind reader." (A staple of late night TV, he was a guest more times than any other person on *The Tonight Show* with Johnny Carson.) In 1988, the Baltimore Orioles started their season by losing their first 21 games in a row. By the 15th loss, many press outlets called on Kreskin to use his powers to break the streak.

Kreskin

Feb. 26, 2001

Dear Seth,

My plan was to spend some time with the team in person to break what had become a mindset, what with the continuous losses. As it turned out I was only able to appear by phone on a radio show urging the fans to concentrate positively on their winning. I am told that cars pulled over to the sides of the roads during the time I set for a mass mental support. Had I gotten the team together at the same time, particularly if I saw them in person, I think I could have broken the slump by impressing on them a tremendous positive belief in their winning.

As for baseball in the year 2101 and to follow: I seriosly believe it would be tragic if the sport were narrowed only to high paying ticketed audiences or to pay television. The American Sport, without any violence or greed, can give its fans a truly mystical experience. ESPecially, Kreskin

Kreskin, Inc., P.O. Box 1383, West Caldwell, NJ 07007-1383

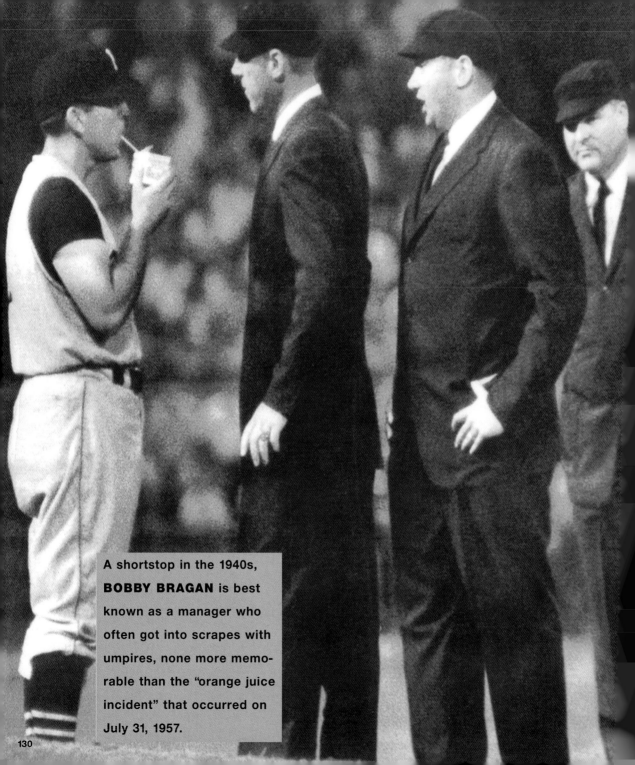

A shortstop in the 1940s, **BOBBY BRAGAN** is best known as a manager who often got into scrapes with umpires, none more memorable than the "orange juice incident" that occurred on July 31, 1957.

Dear Seth:

I had been ejected 3 or 4 times—and always by the same crew of umpires, Stan Landes, Frank Secory + Larry Goetz.

A month earlier, Ron Kline was pitching for us "Pittsburgh Pirates." He disagreed with some calls by umpire Landes. He took some steps toward home plate and Landes took off his mask and took some steps towards Kline and shouted, "Get back on the mound. I'll call the pitches!"

I came out of the dugout and shouted to Kline—"You do the pitching Ronnie—and Stan—you do the umpiring!"

And with that, Landes looked at me and shouted "And you, Bragan, take a shower!" which I did.

So now we are playing in Milwaukee and Lew "Spitball" Burdette is pitching for the Braves—I instructed our players to ask plate umpire Landes to <u>look at the ball</u> when Burdette made his first pitch to each batter. Johnny O'Brien, the leadoff batter, asked umpire Landes to look at the ball.

Dick Groat, the second hitter asked the ump to look at the ball "for saliva." Roberto Clemente the 3rd batter did the same thing—and when Landes looked at the ball he stepped toward me and yelled—"He's not doctoring the ball <u>Bragan</u> so let's play ball and stop protesting about the pitches!"

I started to walk toward Landes when Goetz said "Come on Bobby—let's play ball it looks like rain."

I said "I'm not concerned about the rain—I'm concerned about the spit balls!"

"You're not concerned about the rain?" he shouted. "Then take a hike!"

That was too much. I told my coach to get me a hot dog + cold drink—I was going to find out what this crew had against me. That's when I took the orange drink to the mound and offered a sip to them—oddly I was fired the next day.

Funny—eh? *Bobby Bragan*

Since breaking in with the St. Louis Cardinals in 1989, **TODD ZEILE** has hit more than 233 home runs (and counting) and driven in more than a thousand runs. Currently the third baseman for the Colorado Rockies, Todd is related to some very important figures in United States history.

12-10-01

Dear Seth,

I recall being told at a very young age by my grandmother that she, and subsequently, I were direct descendants of two former United States Presidents: John Adams and John Quincy Adams. I also recall thinking that it was "pretty cool", to be directly related to the Adam's Family (not to be confused with Gomez and Morticia) but nowhere as cool as my buddy whose grandfather animated the Flinstone's cartoon for Hanna Barberra. After all, could John Adams compare to having a grand-father who could whip out Fred Flinstone, George Jetson, or Scooby Doo in one fluid stroke of the pen?

John Adams, second U.S. president (1797–1801).

This past year, that appreciation grew when I was fortunate enough to join a few of my teammates in our nation's capital. As I walked the halls of the West Wing and toured the inner sanctuary of our nations' government, I found myself more and more intrigued with the lives and impact of my presidential lineage. During the tour, we visited the original Senate Building, which now is a monument gallery.

On the floor of the Senate is a brass plaque with only the name "John Quincy Adams". Obviously intrigued, I asked our guide if he knew the genesis of the plaque. He said that during his tenure, Quincy always maintained his seat on that exact spot.

He then noted that Quincy was also notorious for resting his head on his desk and sleeping during Senate sessions. A bit disappointed, I asked if there was more to the story. With a smile, our guide asked me

John Quincy Adams, sixth U.S. president (1825–1829).

134

to stand on the plaque and face away from the majority of the room. He then explained to me that the Senate floor, as it is today, was split by Party affiliation, and that Quincy had the furthest desk from the opposing party.

Our guide then proceeded to walk to the opposite side of the Senate floor and whisper with his back to me. To my amazement, I could clearly understand every word. The marble floors and ceiling created a "whispering arch" which funneled directly to the spot in which Quincy's desk stood for years. He made a practice of eavesdropping on partisan issues and keeping a step ahead. Resourceful or deceitful? Either way, the Adams Family legacy has proven to be one of the most innovative and influential in the history of our nation and thus has become a growing point of pride in my own family.

Sincerely, Todd Zeile

On November 2, 1974, Milwaukee outfielder **DAVE MAY** was traded for Hank Aaron, baseball's all-time home run king.

Seth

When I heard I was traded for Hank Aaron, I was in a Chicago hotel, watching Wide World of Sports. At first I shocked, I left the meetings I had in Chicago for home in Milwaukee. The thing of being traded for Hank, just so he can finish his career there, in milwaukee didn't rub too smooth with me, because I wasn't just a throw in player. If I played right away when I got to Atlanta, I would've felt better about it. I had a manager who thought Hank was still there. I didn't play until they changed managers, I spent two long wasteless years in Atlanta. But now, when your career is long over. And your part of a question, its a part of your baseball career you can add to your stats.

Da

136

JOEL YOUNGBLOOD woke up on August 4, 1982, not knowing that he was about to experience the craziest day (and night) that a player has ever known.

Seth,

So it's Saturday morning... we started the game at 1:05. I was with the Mets and we were playing the Cubs. It was the 4th inning at Wrigley Field, and Joe Torre, my manager, called me over when we were in the dugout and told me that he was taking me out of the game.

I said, "Joe, why are you taking me out of the game? I already have a double and knocked in a couple of runs" (which turned out to be the game-winning runs – off Hall of Famer Ferguson Jenkins, no less!) Joe told me, the reason he was pulling me was because I had just literally been traded by the Mets to the Montreal Expos. He had to take me out because I wasn't a Met anymore.

Montreal was short of players so they asked if the Mets could send me immediately (the Expos were playing in Philadelphia).

What happened next was a total whirlwind: I quickly said goodby to my teammates in the clubhouse, took off my uniform, took a shower, packed my baseball equipment, got in a cab, went to my hotel, packed my clothes, checked out of the hotel made reservations to fly to Philadelphia and got back in the cab and headed for the airport. As I got into the taxicab ready to take me to O'Hare, I realized I made a terrible mistake: I left my glove on the dugout steps at Wrigley Field.

I had packed everything but my glove. My glove at that time was more important than the flight. Because I had used this glove for, like, 14 years. So, back to Wrigley,

2:09 p.m.

2:27 p.m.

3:31 p.m.

3:37 p.m.

where I ran inside, picked my glove up, told my now ex-teammates "bye" again, ran outside, got in the cab and sprinted to the plane to Philly, barely making it.

When I landed in Philly, I called a cab, waited for my bags, just like a regular tourist, and went to Veterans Stadium, where it was the eighth inning of the game there between the Phillies and my new team the Montreal Expos. This all happened so fast!

8:34 p.m.

I went inside the clubhouse, put my new uniform on, walked into the Expos dugout. And before I knew it, I was called into the game as a pinch hitter. This time I would be facing another great Hall-of-Famer to be, Steve Carlton. And wouldn't you know, I got a base hit off "Lefty" too. The next day I wake up and an article in the paper said that I was the only player in Major League Baseball history to have two hits playing for two different teams in two different cities in one day.

9:23 p.m.

9:30 p.m.

9:34 p.m.

And I'm pretty sure I used the same baseball bat for both hits!

All the best Seth, Jeff Youngblood

139

Dear Seth,

I was very upset before "the play" occurred. Because I had just "booted" a routine double-play ball. So if you believe in fate, The triple play would not have occurred if I hadn't made this error.

Omar Olivares works Shane Spencer to a full count. As he (Omar) delivers his 3-2 pitch I notice the runners, (Jorge Posada on first & Tino Martinez on second) moving on the ~~then~~ pitch. Just then, Shane hits a soft line drive to right where I was playing him, SHADE up the middle. I catch it, tag second, then Jorge. History! Routine triple-play! If there's such a thing. HA.

Being a veteran on this team has definitely tested my patience level. But its worked good for both parties. Instead of me being so introverted, I'm opening up to these kids. With 13 plus yrs. of experience at the major league level I've seen a lot. So I take it upon myself to help Anyway possible. Such As defensive set ups, opposing pitchers tendencies and yes, umpires. ~~Where they~~ What zone's each has.

I'm not big on vocal leadership. To me, action carries more weight. But if I'm HARD pressed, HEADS WILL TURN!

Sincerely,

Gary Sheffield
†

4/11/2000

Dear Mr. SWIRSKY,

Dizzy was throwing every off speed type pitch, you could think of, in other words a lot of junk - not enough to hit but enough to fool. I didn't get a hit off him.

We were all having a good time and enjoying every minute of it. No player ever thought Dizzy was trying to show them up; it was a thrill to bat against him. There will never be another Dizzy Dean.

Sincerely,

Floyd Baker

The mitt Dizzy used that day.

Long before there were shortstops named A-Rod, Nomar, Jeter, Ripken, Banks, and Tejada, there was Honus Wagner, who starred for the Pittsburgh Pirates from 1897 to 1917 and was one of the five original inductees into baseball's Hall of Fame (along with Babe Ruth, Ty Cobb, Christy Mathewson, and Walter Johnson). His extremely rare 1909 baseball card is one of the most highly sought-after pieces of memorabilia (one sold in 2000 for $1.25 million).

LESLIE WAGNER BLAIR is his granddaughter.

WAGNER, PITTSBURG

Leslie Wagner Blair

Dear Seth,

Today when a person hears the words, Honus Wagner, most think of the world famous baseball trading card. My grandfather would be embarrassed with all the hype placed on a piece of paper bearing his likeness. The reason he had the cards pulled from the T206 baseball card set was that he loved children and he did not want them to have to buy tobacco in order to have his cards. I was excited to see for what the card finally sold. And, No, I do not have one. I wish I had!

"When I was a small boy in Kansas, a friend of mine and I went fishing, and as we sat there in the warmth of a summer afternoon on a riverbank, we talked about what we wanted to do when we grew up. I told him that I wanted to be a real major league ballplayer, a real professional like Honus Wagner. My friend said he'd like to be the president of the United States. Neither of us got our wish."

—Dwight D. Eisenhower

In his spare time, Buck loved to fish. I remember my mother, Betty telling me Dwight Eisenhower wanted to meet with Buck. But, Buck was going fishing that day. It wasn't that he didn't want to see Ike, but it was Buck's day to fish! So, Ike's entire entourage went out to the "watering hole" and for a while those two talked and fished!

Even decades after my grandfather retired to the great "diamond in the sky," I still remember him fondly. When people ask me what I got from him, I can truly say, Love and memories, but NOT his bow legs!   Leslie Wagner Blair

When **GOOSE GOSSAGE**, the dominant relief pitcher for the New York Yankees (310 lifetime saves), got Carl Yastrzemski to hit into a game-ending pop-up in the nail-biting one-game playoff between the Yankees and the Boston Red Sox on October 2, 1978, Yankees fans were both relieved and excited—until third baseman Graig Nettles looked as if he were about to miss the ball.

Seth,

 I did see Nettles catch many pop-ups throughout our times together. But I had never really watched that closely where he caught the ball. On this particular pop-up, I watched every second of it.

 When it finally reached Nettles' glove, I was watching for the catch to be made with arms extended, but instead, his glove was next to his shoulder.

 For a split second my heart kinda' stopped, for I thought he had missed it. Whew!

"Goose"

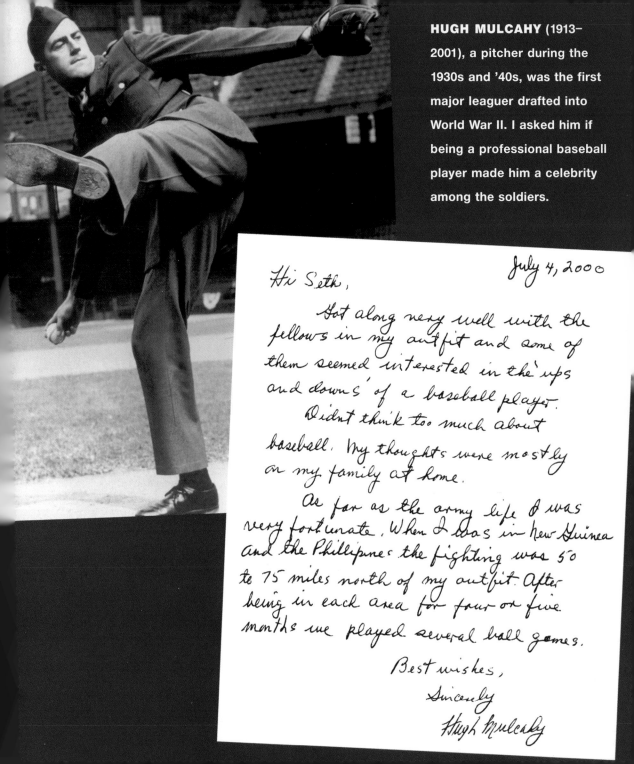

HUGH MULCAHY (1913–2001), a pitcher during the 1930s and '40s, was the first major leaguer drafted into World War II. I asked him if being a professional baseball player made him a celebrity among the soldiers.

July 4, 2000

Hi Seth,

Got along very well with the fellows in my outfit and some of them seemed interested in the 'ups and downs' of a baseball player.

Didn't think too much about baseball. My thoughts were mostly on my family at home.

As far as the army life I was very fortunate. When I was in New Guinea and the Phillipines the fighting was 50 to 75 miles north of my outfit. After being in each area for four or five months we played several ball games.

Best wishes,

Sincerly

Hugh Mulcahy

Ray Chapman was the popular shortstop for the Cleveland Indians from 1912 to 1920. On August 16, 1920, he was hit in the head by a Carl Mays pitch and died hours later of his injury—the only major league player to be killed on a big-league field. I asked his 97-year-old sister **MARGARET JOY** if she could tell me what kind of man her brother was.

2-10-2001

Dear Seth,

about my brother, Ray; I could write reams about him. Besides being an athlete, he was real "arty". He was very musical - could sing beautifully and whistle like a charm. The neighbors always said they knew when he was home because they could hear him whistling. He was so high-spirited and such a joy to be around. He just lit up the place!

When in New York, he would attend all his good friend Al Jolson's performances; also the Follies.

After a ballgame in St. Louis, there was a little boy selling newspapers at the train. Ray said, "Whose boy are you Cal," and the boy replied, "Chappy's boy!" Then Ray threw him some money. That was typical of my brother. He was so personable and so caring.

As to his untimely death, it was a tragedy for our family. My family did not get the message that Ray had been hurt. Only a telegram that he was dead. My Mother collapsed and had to have Doctor Care. We were devestated! He had been so wonderful to my parents and my brother and Me.

Just a word about the funeral service. It was in the Cathedral downtown. Such a crowd. They had to make way for us to get into the church - Men tipped their hats as the Casket was carried into the building. The choir sang a lovely rendition of Lord Kindly Light. Strange that I would remember that.

Seth, that's my story as I remember it. I appreciate the fact that you are interested in my brother. He was a true gentleman and you would have loved knowing him. God bless.

— Margaret (Chapman) Joy

151

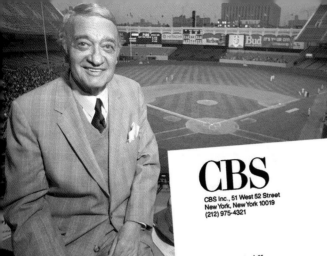

WALTER CRONKITE (pictured below), the most respected and influential newsman of his time, wrote this letter to Mel Allen (1913–1996), the longtime "voice of the New York Yankees" (1939–1964). Allen, known for his phrase "How about that!", was the first broadcaster (along with his contemporary Red Barber) to be enshrined in baseball's Hall of Fame in 1978.

CBS

CBS Inc., 51 West 52 Street
New York, New York 10019
(212) 975-4321

Mr. Mel Allen
c/o The New York Athletic Club
180 Central Park South
New York City

November 11, 1993

Dear Mel:

A previous engagement keeps me from being with you but please accept these congratulations for your induction into Alabama's Hall of Fame.

I'll never forget our first meeting at Yankee Stadium a few decades ago when you came out of the radio booth and greeted my host, the late, great Rex Smith. A horde of young boys besieged you for your autograph, gracefully given, and then turned to me. I was flattered until I heard one of them say to the other: "Who the hell is he?"

Your career has been an inspiration to a couple of generations of young sports reporters and broadcasters. And to me.

Walter Cronkite

DEAR SETH,

The first Major league game I went to was at Chavez Ravine to see the Dodgers. I will surely remember the first game I take my son Chase to see. I will be playing in it!

I enjoy watching games very much because I can relax and enjoy it. That is my biggest challenge today — enjoying the time I spend in baseball. Sometimes I get so caught up in performing and having success that I forget to enjoy myself.

My # 1 quote about baseball — describes it to a 'T' for me: "Baseball can bring me the ultimate pleasure — It can also cause me the ultimate pain." In a word, Sweet-n-Sour. I just made it one word.

sincerely,

Gabriel Kapler

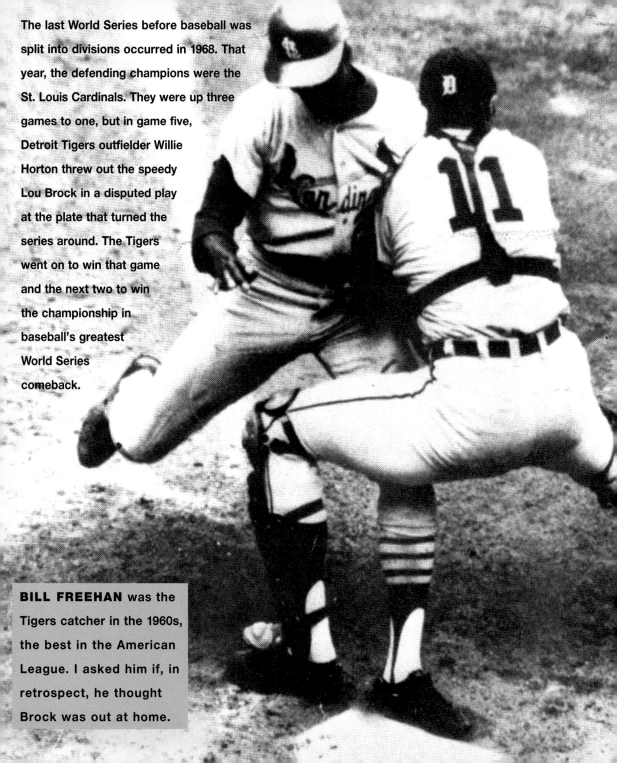

The last World Series before baseball was split into divisions occurred in 1968. That year, the defending champions were the St. Louis Cardinals. They were up three games to one, but in game five, Detroit Tigers outfielder Willie Horton threw out the speedy Lou Brock in a disputed play at the plate that turned the series around. The Tigers went on to win that game and the next two to win the championship in baseball's greatest World Series comeback.

BILL FREEHAN was the Tigers catcher in the 1960s, the best in the American League. I asked him if, in retrospect, he thought Brock was out at home.

Seth:

Doug Harvey took his time to see if I held on to the ball — as Lou tried to run me over instead of sliding. If you look at the films you will see him come back and try to "re-touch" home plate — I then re-touched him.

He maintains that — why should I touch him a 2nd time if I had done it the first time. My response was: why were you coming back to touch it again if you touched it the 1st time.

However all the above is moot! Check the "Box scores" and that is the only real criteria — "the ump said out!" How many HISTORICAL sports events have been decided on swap decisions by officials.

I have looked at the photo's and replays a million times and no one can tell conclusively what happened.

The result — It was close! The ump called him out! The series took a turn and I've got a 1968 World Series Ring that says "1968 World Champions".

By the way — Lou Brock is a great guy — a good friend and we have re-enacted this play numerous times at "Old-Timers Games."

My Best!

155

March 9, 2000

Ernie Harwell
Tiger Broadcaster

Dear Seth:

Because I was a song writer, Tiger GM Jim Campbell appointed me to select anthem singers for '68 World Series. For first two games in Detroit I picked Margaret Whiting and Marvin Gaye.

A friend in record business told me that José Feliciano had thrilled the Greek Theater audience in Hollywood with his rendition of the anthem.

José agreed to come + sing for the 5th game. His performance caused an uproar. The NY Times printed his photo on page one as he strummed his guitar and sang in center field.

It was a watermark in anthem singing. He rendered a soulful, haunting version.

I think the uproar came because
1) It was different
2) Jose was singing in midst of troubled times and because the Guitar was identified with the "hippie" movement.
3) many fans felt he had long hair — another hippy characteristic.

I almost lost my job because of the uproar. But I stood up for Jose and took blame for the selection.

Best wishes — Ernie Harwell

Fans Protest Soul Singer's Anthem Version

DETROIT, Oct. 7 (AP)—A blind Puerto Rican soul-music singer now living in Newport Beach, Calif., started a storm of protests when he sang the National Anthem before the fifth game of the World Series between the St. Louis Cardinals and the Detroit Tigers today.

Twenty-three-year-old José Feliciano, whose rendition of the anthem differed greatly from its usual formal strains, was booed by many in the crowd of 53,634.

His rendition was done in a slower beat, similar to a blend between soul and folk singing styles. He accompanied himself on the guitar.

The performance caused consternation and criticism among television viewers throughout the nation. Newspapers and radio and television stations were flooded with calls. A newspaper in St. Petersburg, Fla., said it was overwhelmed by calls from persons protesting vehemently about the singing.

A spokesman for the National Broadcasting Company in New York, which televised the game, said that both New York and Hollywood, Calif., network stations also received a rash of calls from irate viewers. The New York office received 400 calls.

N.B.C. noted that Feliciano was hired by the Detroit Tigers and a spokesman for the network added, "We just covered it, that's all."

Although Feliciano declined to label his version of the National Anthem, he said it reflected, "the way I feel."

"I just do my thing—what I feel," said Feliciano, seated behind first base with his seeing-eye dog, Trudy, and his wife, Hilda.

"I was a little scared when I was asked to sing the anthem," Feliciano said. "I was afraid people would misconstrue it and say I'm making fun of it. But I'm not. It's the way I feel."

Feliciano has been singing for six years. He was invited to sing the anthem by Ernie Harwell, the Tigers play-by-play broadcaster who also writes music.

"I picked him because he's

Associated Press

José Feliciano, blind Puerto Rican singer, singing his version of National Anthem in Detroit yesterday. The rendition was part of ceremonies that preceded fifth Series game.

one of the outstanding singers in America today," Harwell said. "I had heard from people in music whose opinion I respect that he had an interesting version of the National Anthem."

Explaining how he devised his version of the anthem, Feliciano, blind since birth, said:

"America is young now, and I thought maybe the anthem could be revived now. This country has given me many opportunities. I owe everything I have to this country. I wanted to contribute something to this country, express my gratification for what it has done for me."

Feliciano has recorded such popular hits as "Light My Fire" and "High Heeled Sneakers." He left in the fifth inning to return to Las Vegas, Nev., where he is currently appearing.

Tony Kubek, a television broadcaster and former shortstop with the New York Yankees, said he liked Feliciano's rendition.

"I think he did one heckuva job," said Kubek. "I've seen him before and he's one of the top folk guitarists in the country. I feel the youth of America has to be served and this is the type of music they want."

Many others in Tiger

Stadium did not like the rendition.

"I thought he was very good," said Michael Jordan, a fan from Boston. "It's hard to say why you like it, but it seems to bring out a little more than the regular versions."

"I'm young enough to understand it, but I think it stunk " said Joe Oyler of Marion, Ind., the brother of Ray Oyler, a Tiger infielder. "It was nonpatriotic."

"It was a disgrace, an insult," said Mrs. Arlene Raicevich of Detroit. "I'm going to write to my Senator about it."

STEVE SWIRSKY is my father. A standout base-ball and basketball player at Hillhouse High School in New Haven and at Dartmouth College in the late 1950s and early '60s, he remains my all-time favorite guy.

August 11, 2001

Dear Seth:

You used to love to hear this story when you were growing up. In the mid-1950's, after years in Little League, I played in the Babe Ruth League. At 13, I was selected for the All-Star team to compete for the Conn. State championship with my melting-pot team: Italian and Irish kids from "the hill" section of New Haven, black kids from the Dixwell Ave section and Jews from Westville, the small suburb where I lived.

We all thought we'd be the next Joe DiMaggio or Willie Mays and winning the state title definitely fueled that fantasy. We went on to the New England championship in Cranston, R.I., winning the first two games in the round-robin single-loss elimination. In the final game we were trailing 7-2, with 2 out in the bottom of the last inning. Things looked so bleak that I took off my spikes and resigned myself to the long bus ride home. My coach told me to put them back on. "We still have a shot!" he said. What followed was a baseball miracle: two walks, an error, a double, a hit batter and two singles. The game was now 7-6 with two outs and my turn at bat. Our opponent had simply run out of gas — and heart! In an entire lifetime, a few days stand out — this was one of mine.

With bases loaded, I drilled the first pitch into right-centerfield to win the game 8-7. Revved from our come from behind victory, our team took a cross-country train to the BABE RUTH WORLD SERIES in Portland, Oregon - full of optimism and a burning desire to win.

It wasn't long before reality set back in. The first pitcher we faced was future legend Mickey Lolich, only 15 at the time but, even then clearly destined for the Majors.

I was the clean-up hitter and he struck me out three times with only ten pitches. We lost 8-0. I didn't do much better against future Yankee star AL DOWNING. The message was unmistakable: You're good - but not that good! That dose of reality was an important lesson for those of us not fated to be in the "bigs."

Baseball is a great teacher of sportsmanship, endurance, focus, patience, respect for teammates and coaches and what the essence of fu𝐍 is all about.

Love,
Dad

The patch from my dad's 1955 All-Star uniform.

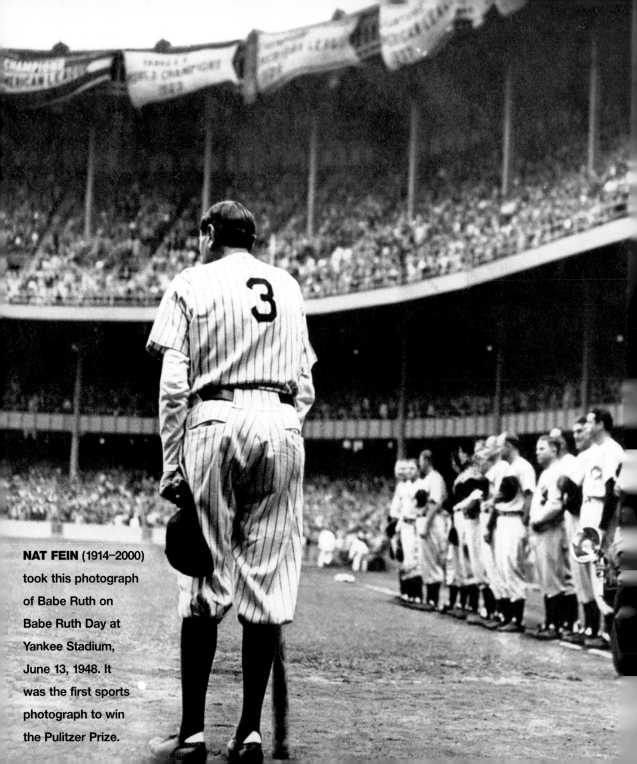

NAT FEIN (1914–2000) took this photograph of Babe Ruth on Babe Ruth Day at Yankee Stadium, June 13, 1948. It was the first sports photograph to win the Pulitzer Prize.

Dear Seth,   8-28-99

It was a gloomy day at Yankee Stadium,
Babe Ruth was making his final appearance after years
of playing baseball. Thousands of fans had jammed
the stadium to say goodbye to Ruth.

The Babe came out of the dugout, waving
and walked slowly to homeplate. The band began to
play "Auld Lang Syne". It was a tremendous emotional
experience. George Herman Ruth stepped forward. No
one could mistake that figure. His wide shoulders
slightly stooped as he leaned on his baseball bat
to steady himself. the crowd rose in tribute to
the man who was the idol of Millions. they had

Twenty-five photographers were there
covering the Babe. none of the photos I made told
the story. The fact that Babe Ruth's Number 3
would never be used again had to be included
so I left the other photographers and walked around
Ruth. Then I saw it- The Composition that told
the story in one picture, the "Babe Bows out."
Luck was with me.

                                                    Nat Fein

161

Transcripts

GEORGE BUSH *(pp. 2–3)*

1-24-02

Dear Seth—

Baseball has always given me "something to write home about."

I'll never forget the spring of 1948 when Babe Ruth came to Yale Field. I was Captain of Yale's team so I got to go on the field to receive some papers from the Babe. Riddled with throat cancer he could barely speak. But it was his very commanding presence that I'll never forget. Bent over, his body wasted, he was still the great Babe Ruth that every baseball loving kid in America wanted to emulate.

I had a lot of wonderful moments as Vice President and as President—great seats at great events; but the Babe at Yale topped them all—

George Bush

FLIP SCHULKE *(pp. 4–9)*

A Sunday afternoon with Dr. Martin Luther King, Jr. and his baseball son, Marty.

Occasionally, when in Atlanta, on a Sunday, I would go to Ebenezer Baptist Church, to hear Dr. King speak.

Afterwards he would invite me to his house for one of Coretta's great chicken feasts.

I never took photographs. We both would rather talk and he, play with the kids.

When I got out of my car that Sunday, he told me to bring my cameras, I asked "Why"— and he replied, "It's not every day one learns that one has won the Nobel Peace Prize."

We had lunch in the dining room, where a picture of Gandhi looked down on the family.

After lunch, the kids went to the back yard to play—as they usually did on a Sunday afternoon.

Yoki in a swing/glider where she could have close, private conversations with her dad.

Dexter liked his dad to push him on his swing.

Bunny was so young, that her favorite play was a mild "rough house" with her dad and especially liked being tossed in the air— squeeling with pleasure all the time—

Marty's favorite was playing baseball with his dad. They worked on the basics of catch and throwing the baseball, but his favorite form of "playing ball" was learning how to "hit." His dad would pitch, underhanded so Marty could learn the "swing" and how to hit.

I had seen this playing baseball many times after Sunday dinners in the past—but this special Sunday I got to record the love and caring exhibited by both Dr. King and the 4 children. A more hands-on father I had rarely seen in my work as a photojournalist.

Dr. King was a great father, family man and a very good baseball coach—

Flip Schulke
March 28, 2002
West Palm Beach, FL.

EDWARD M. KENNEDY *(pp. 10–11)*

(See typed letter.)

GATES BROWN *(pp. 12–13)*

Seth,

We were playing a day game in Detroit & Norm Cash, who wasn't playing that day, & I usually got hot dogs for each other every inning or so.

I knew Manager Mayo Smith didn't usually call on me until the 7th inning but this day he called on me in the 6th inning & as I said Norm & I were on the end of the bench eating them. I couldn't leave them there because I knew when I came back they wouldn't be there. So, I put the hot dogs in my jersey & went up to hit.

Of all the times I didn't care if I got a hit would you believe I hit one up the gap & had to go head-first into second. When I got up, I had mustard & ketchup all over the front of my jersey.

When I got back to the bench, everyone was

laughing like hell, all except Mayo who was livid. He fined me $100 & said the only reason he didn't fine me more was because I wasn't making too much money (smile) end of story.

Gates Brown

JULIA RUTH STEVENS *(pp. 14–15)*
(See typed letter.)

PAUL McCARTNEY *(p. 16)*
Dear Seth,

I became a Yankees fan when my friend Lorne Michaels got seats for us in 2000. It was the first game Heather & I had actually been to! So we became instant fans.

Yeah, it was <u>pretty</u> cool hearing my music played at a game . . . it's just a pity that they didn't win this year, but, if they had to lose, it couldn't have been to a better state—Arizona!

Go Yankees
Cheers!
Paul McCartney

SHAWN GREEN *(pp. 17–19)*
11/1/01
Dear Seth,

As a Jewish player in the Major Leagues, I've had numerous interesting experiences. I've had the pleasure of meeting fascinating people throughout North America who have reached out to me because I am Jewish. There are many Jewish, die-hard baseball fans out there, yet there are few of us out there on the field. One night, however, back in 1996 in Milwaukee, I was not alone. At the time, I was playing for the Toronto Blue Jays. As I walked up to the plate and manicured the dirt in the batter's box before my first at bat, I greeted the catcher, Jesse Levis, and the umpire, Al Clark. This is something I always do my first time to the

plate. I knew Jesse fairly well, and therefore I knew he was also Jewish. I greeted him, "What's up Yid!" and he replied "Not much Yid!" (this was an ongoing joke in reference to us both being Jewish). Meanwhile, strike one goes by me, and Al Clark looks at me and says, "By the way, Happy New Year." I stepped out of the box and said, "Al, you're Jewish?" Jesse replied, "Of course, you didn't know that?" We then proceeded to wish each other "happy new years" and I proceeded to strike out! This is one memory of baseball I will never forget.

Though I didn't grow up in a religious household, I was raised with a strong sense of identity. I was a huge baseball fan, just like lots of kids. At the time I was growing up, there really weren't any well-known Jewish players (at least as far as I knew). I was, however, very aware of Hank Greenberg and Sandy Koufax and the tremendous role models they were for Jewish people everywhere.

As my baseball career progressed, I always remembered the decisions that the two greatest Jewish ballplayers made, and I told myself that if I was ever in a position to, in any way, fill that role, I would. Thus, I feel a strong responsibility to make the right choices when it comes to such topics as not playing on Yom Kippur. I'm not trying to be "the next Greenberg or Koufax," but I am trying to do my part as a Jewish ballplayer.

Sincerely,
Shawn Green

LEONARD GARCIA *(pp. 20–21)*
Dear Seth—

In 1967, we went on a season ending trip to Detroit. Aurilio had just been called up from El Paso. He was <u>19</u> and I was <u>18</u> at the time. During batting practice, I wore uniform #34 and Aurilio wore #37. We were playing catch when a photographer came up and took our picture. We told him he wrote our names down in the wrong order. He must have forgotten to correct the mistake before sending the photos to Topps.

I didn't know why coach Amaro kept calling me 'Aurilio' until one day in 1969, I was in the Angel clubhouse and saw the card. Everyone had a good laugh. Jim Fregosi knew of the mistake all along and thought we did it on purpose. He may have put the photographer up to it.

By the way—I now work for Topps!
Leonard Garcia

ELLIOTT GOULD (pp. 22–25)
Dear Seth,

Our fathers were invincible, all powerful, omnipotent. We depended on them so deeply, that it was inconceivable that they could be fallible or mortal. It was October 3, 1947. The Brooklyn Dodgers were facing the Yankees in game four of the World Series at Ebbet's Field. The unlikely Bums vs. the vaunted Bronx Bombers. My friend Donny Kramer lived across the street on West 9th. I had just turned 9. Donny's father Larry, suddenly and unexpectedly died that day. I asked my mom if I could invite Donny in to listen to the rest of the game with us. The Dodgers were losing 2 to 1. It was the bottom of the ninth, and Floyd Bevens, the Yankee pitcher, was unbelievably hurling a no hitter. There were two out. Brooklyn had two runners on base, Gianfriddo on second and Miksis on first, when Burt Shotton, the Dodger manager put Cookie Lavagetto up to pinch hit for Eddie Stanky. On a one strike pitch, Lavagetto lined a double off the right field wall scoring Gianfriddo and Miksis giving the Dodgers a miraculous victory. It was a magical moment. It transcended the shock, the tragedy, and the loss of my friend's father for a moment, a brief moment, but a

moment none the less, reflecting spirit and hope in the darkest hour.

With love and devotion to all our fathers and mothers, forever, I remain a fan.
Elliott Gould

TOM SEAVER (pp. 26–29)
Seth—

Warming up in the bullpen—Rube Walker, my pitching coach—knew I had exceptional stuff that night vs. the Cubs.

Jimmy Qualls was the one player in the lineup I had never faced and I knew nothing about him. He in fact hit the ball hard all three times he came to the plate. I remember telling myself that if anyone is going to get a hit, it will be Qualls (not withstanding Billy Williams), because I did not know his strengths or weaknesses. I have never seen Qualls since. And I do recall the black cat coming on the field.
Very Best,
Tom Seaver

ERNIE BANKS (pp. 30–31)
(See typed letter.)

ELIZABETH WRIGLEY-FIELD (p. 32)
Dear Seth,

I've always loved having a name people get a kick out of! My mom's last name is Wrigley and my dad's is Field, but they didn't think they could give a kid the last name Wrigley-Field—that would just be too weird, and the kid would probably be teased.

I thought that was ludicrous. I'm not a baseball fan, but I've always loved how excited my name makes people. Plus, the Cubs fans I've met have been a spirited bunch. They seemed like a good group to get associated with because they all seemed to genuinely adore the stadium with my name. So in first grade, my desire to be noticed for a funny name everyone liked combined with my feminist sensibilities (it seemed fairer to have both my parents' names than just my dad's) made me start referring to myself as Elizabeth Wrigley-Field and everyone's called me that since.

I guess people really like my name because it's unique. I'm an only child, and Wrigley and Field (as opposed to Fields) are both uncommon names, so I assume I'm the only person in the world with my last name. Still, I'm holding out for one day meeting an Alex Fenway-Park or something similar. We'll have so many stories to swap!

> Sincerely,
> Elizabeth Wrigley-Field

GAYLORD PERRY *(p. 33)*

Seth,

A writer for the S.F. Examiner paper told <u>Alvin</u> <u>Dark</u> that this kid—Gaylord Perry—will hit some home runs for you.

Alvin said, <u>a man will land on the moon</u> before Gaylord Perry hits a home run.

The day they landed on the moon, I was pitching—about 30 minutes later, I hit my first home run!

> Gaylord

BUZZ ALDRIN *(p. 34)*

Seth—

I've thrown a few first pitches . . . for a minor league team in Iowa, and for the Anaheim Angels in 1999. It sure felt good—but if I were pitching on the moon—it would have floated a lot farther!!

> Buzz Aldrin

RON SWOBODA *(p. 35)*

Dear Seth,

1969 was an incredible year <u>without</u> the Mets winning a World Series. The War, the protests, the social upheaval, the recent assassinations of King and Kennedy, mixed in with the Moon landing an unprecedented good economic times. It seemed like all things were possible and all things were happening simultaneously.

We were young people in a liberal New York and I took my leanings from that. But with the focus you need to play major league baseball I was more insulated from the tumult though certainly not unaware!

> Sincerely,
> Ron Swoboda
> 1969 METS

P.S. YOU ASK TOO LARGE A QUESTION HERE!

PETER TORK *(pp. 36–38)*

Nov. 27, '01

Dear Seth,

After the Monkee phenomenon died down, I knocked around for a while, eventually getting a couple of teaching jobs in the L.A. area through my then wife, who was then an educator herself. One of those two teaching jobs was also to be the baseball coach, at a small prep school in Beverly Hills, an opportunity I jumped at!

It was fascinating and harrowing. I was not yet sober at the time, and while not actually under the influence while at school, I was not, sadly, at my best most of the time, either.

BUT! It remains a high point of my life. I get a huge charge out of telling anybody interested that I was a high school baseball coach, and some of the individual memories rank very high on my top <u>whatever</u> number list.

For instance—The 1st day, I was standing behind third base when the batter lost the bat which came whirligigging at me, full-tilt. I thought: is this a test? Talking batting, pitching, fielding, and so on . . . To be immersed in that role, and to <u>participate</u>—at any level—with the game as it's actually played will stay with me—and very fondly—to the end of my mental life.

One other note—you might think that having a celebrity for a baseball coach would jazz the kids, but I saw very little of that. They called me "coach," as was proper, altho' I might have preferred the more egalitarian "Peter." But, our interactions were all about the game. You know, celebrity disappears very shortly when you're actually there.

Peter Tork

DAVID J. MULLANY *(p. 39)*
November 9, 2001
Dear Seth—

My grandfather, David N. Mullany was born & raised in Hatfield, MA on a tobacco farm.

On his way home from job hunting one day, he noticed my father and his friends playing a game in the backyard with a plastic golf ball and broom handle. It was a highly competitive game needing few players and a limited amount of space.

He and my dad, David A. Mullany, set out to create a plastic ball that would curve controllably with little effort and wouldn't damage property. After several tries, they ended up with a design for the ball we manufacture today with 8 oblong holes on one half.

They named the ball and the game they played "WIFFLE." (In dad's neighborhood a swing and a miss was a "wiff" and the new ball produced lots of them!)

As to your question regarding Wiffle and life in general. . . . I think its simplicity is still appealing. We find ourselves barraged with rules & regulations on a daily basis. We're required to obtain licenses and authorization to conduct just about any activity. Now, I'm not saying that going out and playing Wiffle will solve all (or any) of that but how many games are left where kids, or adults, are the captains of their own ship? How often do <u>you</u> make the rules? A ball hit off the chimney is a home run? OK! It's an out? Fine by me! How many strikes to an out? 1? 2? 7? You decide. It's <u>your</u> backyard. Play any way you want!

Best regards,
David J. Mullany, V.P.

CORNELIUS SAVAGE *(pp. 40–41)*
154081 International
HE PLAYED BASEBALL WHILE LINCOLN WATCHED.

This is Mr. Cornelius Savage, who has the distinction of having played baseball in the backyard of the White House, with President Lincoln as a spectator. Mr. Savage was born in New York, and he remembers many details of the life of the great President.

On one occasion President Lincoln intervened in behalf of several boys who were ordered to stop playing ball on the White House grounds, by the Public Building Officer. The gentleman above happened to be one of the boys.
B-11-21

TIM RUSSERT *(pp. 42–45)*
June 5, 2001
Dear Seth,

I grew up in Buffalo, N.Y. My favorite birthday present was to pile into our 1955 green Chevy station wagon and drive 4 hours to Cleveland for an Indians vs Yankees doubleheader. It was the only major league baseball game I saw all year so I begged to stay to the last out.

I <u>now</u> realize how hard 18 innings and eight hours of driving was on my Dad and my Uncles.

While they had to stay alert on the way home, I slept leaning against the ice chest in the back of the wagon.

My favorite player was Yankee catcher, number 8, Yogi Berra. My dream was to get his autograph or catch his foul ball. Never did. Sitting in the upper level was not conducive to either!

Fast forward 40 years. My son Luke and I are invited to the White House on March 30, 2001 to meet the Hall of Famers.

Within moments I'm talking to Yogi Berra. Then Whitey Ford too. The greatest pitcher-catcher duo of my boyhood.

Eight weeks later, I interviewed Yogi. It was one of the most interesting, fun, and in a remarkable way emotional hours of my life. My life with my Dad—and now with my son—inextricably linked to baseball—and Yogi Berra. Father and son forever. And yes—I got Yogi's autograph. So did Luke. And we got one for my Dad too.

Tim Russert

P.S. Luke thanked President Bush for inviting him to the White House and showing him the Oval Office. He seemed to suggest he might have a chance for the Hall of Fame and The Presidency! Very funny—but I will never get in the way of a 15 year old's dreams. After all I met Yogi Berra—in the White House.

GEORGE W. BUSH *(pp. 46–49)*
Dear Seth,

The season is close, and I am ready for opening day. I will be throwing out the first pitch this year (probably a cut fast ball) in Milwaukee. What an honor to do so as the President.

I love baseball. My affection must have had its start when I watched the '48 Yale Bulldogs practice and play the game. My Dad was on first; Mother, the scorekeeper.

It grew in West Texas as a little leaguer (catcher for the Cubs) and as a tossing

companion with #41 (President G HW Bush). I still remember catching his left-handed throws.

I remember my hero, Willie Mays, my first game in the Astrodome (Morgan hit a homer), and being introduced as a General Partner of the Texas Rangers.

I treasure my memories of the great game and look forward to collecting a lot more of them starting soon.

Best regards,
George W. Bush

RICHIE SCHEINBLUM *(p. 50)*
(See typed letter.)

BUCK O'NEIL *(p. 51)*
Being the 1st Black coach in the M.L. was bitter sweet for me. Sweet because I was with the Big League team, but bitter because I knew men who were capable to coach & manage in the M.L. seventy five years ago.

Buck O'Neil

MO VAUGHN *(pp. 52–53)*
To Seth,

I think it's a tremendous honor to wear #42 in N.Y.C. I have always stated that this is not my number, I just wear it to keep a legacy alive.

Jackie Robinson was the man that changed this country and its history forever.

His struggle gave all minorities an opportunity to shine in every sports venue. Every man, woman and child can benefit from his story!

I would hope to be half the man Jackie Robinson was and all he represented. That would be a successful and productive life!

Mo Vaughn

BUD SELIG *(pp. 54–55)*
(See typed letter.)

ED RENDELL *(pp. 56–57)*
Dear Seth:

As Mayor of Philadelphia from 1992–2000, I had the opportunity to meet and work with many heroes—police and firefighters who risked their lives everyday, teachers who worked for low pay because they were dedicated to improving children's lives and ordinary moms and dads who struggle to make a better future for their children.

Of the many heroes I met, however, one embodies this spirit. His name is Michael Springer, a Vietnam veteran, who was walking down the street when he saw a baby perched on the third floor window ledge of a neighborhood rowhouse. Realizing the baby was in danger, Mr. Springer planted himself on the sidewalk below. Just seconds later, the baby fell out of the window, but Mr. Springer caught it and saved it. He truly made the "Catch of a Lifetime." We celebrated Mr. Springer's heroism in City Hall. Rawlings Sporting Goods makes and presents the annual "Gold Glove" awards to baseball players for being the best fielders at their position. They awarded him a Gold Glove for his "great catch," the only time they gave one to a non-player. It was a great day for our city—to honor a great everyday hero like Michael Springer.

Sincerely yours,
Ed Rendell

MEL HARDER *(p. 58)*
Dear Seth:

It was difficult to pick-up the ball from that height. Frank Pytlack missed a couple but then finally he caught one.

Then, the Indians 2nd string catcher Hank Helf caught one so we were proud that two of our catchers were able to catch a ball thrown off the Terminal Tower. It was difficult to do.

Regards
Mel Harder

JIM CAMPANIS *(p. 59)*
Seth,

A little background—my Dad and I were with the Dodger organization at the same time—but never at the same level. When I was in the minor league, he was Vice Pres. in charge of scouting. When I was in the major leagues he was Vice Pres. in charge of both scouting & minor leagues until Dec 13th 1968. I think it was a Friday.

Mr. O'Malley named my Dad General Manager in charge of player personel—15 min. later I was traded to K.C. Royals for $150,000 and two players. He told me that if he was named G.M. it would be a hard decision to make—he waited 15 minutes to trade me. In his defense—I got a big raise to play for K.C. Also the Dodgers had two young catchers in Double and Triple A named Joe Ferguson and Steve Yeager.

But I think I'm still the only player that was traded by his Dad

Jim Campanis

P.S. My Dad died on Father's Day.

TONY SAUNDERS *(pp. 60–61)*
Seth,

So many thoughts race thru my mind as I know that I have to walk away from a game that I love so much. The hardest part of the whole thing is letting go of something that I have worked so hard to get. There are also other thoughts that enter my mind. What am I going to do for the rest of my life, hell I'm only 26 years old? Do I write out a formal retirement letter or do I just speak from the heart? Those are tough questions for me to have to answer right now, but they have to be done and answered. I guess I will just speak from the heart as I did everytime I stepped out on the mound and went to battle for my teammates. I feel as if there is a huge chunk of my heart missing with nothing to fill it. I have dedicated my whole life to a dream and now it is time to let it go. But it is also another opportunity and a new beginning for whatever it may be . . .

Tony Saunders
#31

BOB COSTAS (pp. 62–65)
Dear Seth,

Here's how I recall the scene late in Game 6 of the '86 World Series: when the Red Sox got 2 in the top of the 10th, NBC dispatched me to their clubhouse for the post game. As the Mets came up in their half, plastic was already covering the Red Sox lockers, champagne was at the ready, the championship trophy was wheeled in on a special cloth-covered stand, and next came the very frail Mrs. Jean Yawkey, well into her eighties escorted by Commissioner Ueberroth, anticipating the first Bosox title since she was a girl.

I stood on a platform constructed for the post game with a monitor in front of me and an earpiece providing me with Vin Scully's play by play.

I was thinking not only of the specific questions I might ask about this Series, and this season, but what might be appropriate to say concerning this first Red Sox World Series triumph in 68 years.

Then Carter singled with two out. Mitchell followed with a hit. I asked Mike Weisman, our executive producer, "What do I do if the Mets tie it?" "If that happens, get the hell out as fast as you can!"

After Knight's fisted single and the wild pitch to Wilson, the game was tied. You could feel Shea Stadium rocking. Mrs. Yawkey, head down, saying nothing, was gently escorted away. I took out the earpiece.

Technicians began dismantling the set-up. Clubhouse men ripped the plastic off the lockers, all accomplished as quickly as a set change at a Broadway show.

By the time Wilson's grounder got by Buckner, the last camera had been rolled out into the corridor.

I was the last to leave, coming out the clubhouse door just as the first of the Red Sox traipsed down the tunnel from the dugout. Many appeared ashen-faced; but maybe that was my imagination.

This much I know for sure—there was total silence until someone, I'm not sure who, smashed a bat against the wall of the tunnel and bellowed a single expletive. There was silence again after that.

That scene remains as dramatic and vivid and human as any scenes of triumph I've ever witnessed.

Bob Costas

MOOKIE WILSON (pp. 66–67)
Dear Seth,

There were a few lessons to be learned from the 86 World Series. Always hustle and give your best. Some say it was luck that Bill Buckner missed that ball I hit, but I believe you make your own luck, because if I had not been running hard down the firstbase line, things might have turned out different. In other words, my hustle caused the error.

So remember, never give up and always

hustle and give it your best, not only in sports but in everything you do because great things happen when you do.

Mookie Wilson

MAX FRAZEE *(pp. 68–69)*
Seth,

There was no "curse of the Bambino." It was just a good business decision as well as a myth portrayed in the press to keep the fans believing it was "Big Harry's" fault rather than the Boston team.

In 1993, I received a call from the Boston Red Sox to come to Fenway Park to receive a World Series pin, which was never given to the club and its members for the 1918 World Series victory. When I arrived, the Red Sox treated me very well. We had a few good laughs, though it was a bit ironic, giving a pin to the most hated man in the history of the Boston Red Sox.

The Sox were playing Kansas City that day and the ceremony would be before the game. All the parties were lined up on the 1st base line near the Boston dugout to receive the pin. When they started to pass the pins to the individuals before me, the fans applauded. When they got to me I was received by 35,000 booing fans. In many ways this is what I expected. After all the boo's settled down, I was smiling and saying to myself, "If only the fans really knew the truth about Big Harry, I doubt they would have booed."

Max Frazee

PAUL GIORGIO *(pp. 70–71)*
Dear Seth,

I attempted to reverse the "curse of the Bambino" by taking it to new heights. I climbed Mount Everest in 2000 and met a Tibetian Holy man called a "Lama". After I came home in the fall of 2000 and saw the New York Yankees win yet another World Series title, I turned to my wife and said that I'm going to visit "the Lama" in 2001 and see if there's anything I can do to "Reverse the Curse."

So on my 2001 Everest Expedition I visited with the lama and he advised me to get the Boston Red Sox cap blessed at base camp ceremony called a "Pujar." After that ceremony I needed to place the cap on the Summit of Everest.

After those 2 procedures took place I was to burn a New York Yankees cap in the pujar fireplace as an "Offering to the Gods." Well I completed the cycle to break the curse and can only hope the Boston Red Sox win the World Series.

Sincerely Yours,
Paul Giorgio

BABE RUTH *(pp. 72–73)*
(See typed letter.)

BOB MALLON *(pp. 74–75)*
July 26, 1949
Dear Mom & Pop

Say Dad you ought to be down here it is really delightfully cool. They say they are having the funniest weather they ever had here in Kansas. But it has really been nice and cool.

I room with Mantle, the shortstop. He was hitting .230 a week and a half ago, he went on a hitting streak and jumped up to .300 in that time. He is fast as lightning, hits and bunts. I'll close for now.

Love,
Bob

P.S. The mosquitoes chew you to death down here, I never saw so many.

BOB SHEPPARD *(p. 76)*

The last time I saw Mickey Mantle was a few months before his death.

I introduced him on "Good Morning, America."

He told the interviewer that he got "goose pimples" every time I announced his name.

So did I!

Players don't correct me when I pronounce their names. That's because I go to them and ask how their names should be pronounced.

That's my job!

You asked for a poem. Here's one I wrote 15 minutes after Roger hit 61:

"Roger Maris Says His Prayers"
They've been pitching me low,
They've been pitching me tight.
I've grown so nervous, tense and pallid.
But my prayers are full of joy to-night—
Thank you, Lord, for Tracy Stallard.
                    Bob Sheppard

EDDIE LAYTON *(p. 77)*

Dear Seth:

During the week, I am in the recording studios making TV and radio commercials. A limo takes me to Yankee Stadium around 4 or 5 PM. At that time, I have my dinner in the Press room. After the game, the limo takes me home.

I love baseball but I hate rain delays and extra innings.

When the Yankees are away, I spend time on my boat which is docked in Tarrytown on the Hudson river.

I am looking forward to another 35 years of playing the organ here—then I'm getting out of the bisness.

                    All the best,
                    Eddie Layton

JOEY LAURICE *(pp. 78–79)*

(See typed letter.)

RALPH BRANCA *(pp. 80–83)*

Dear Seth,

There are things I remember about Oct. 3, 1951 and others "we simply choose to forget."

Before the game I remember kidding with Pee Wee Reese and Jackie Robinson about having "butterflies." An expression used by ballplayers to denote nervousness.

I was designated to be the first pitcher out of the bullpen, even though I had pitched eight innings two days earlier on Monday, Oct. 1st. My arm was very stiff, so I started to throw in the sixth inning to be sure I would have enough time to get loose. Actually, I lob-tossed from forty to forty-five just to get loose.

My arm eventually loosened up so I was able to throw very well and in reality I believe at full strength.

I don't remember the walk in from the bullpen, but I do remember meeting Pee Wee and Jackie on the infield grass and asking "Anyone got butterflies?"

The first pitch I threw was dead center and Thomson took it for a strike. The next pitch was up and in, and about chin high, and Bobby jumped on it. He hit it with an uppercut swing which promotes overspin. I remember saying or praying "sink—sink." Of course, it did sink, but not enough and cleared the wall.

That made baseball history!!

In 1954, when I first learned how the Giants had stolen the signs from the sanctity of their lockerroom and used an electronic device to transmit the signs, I was astonished!! I also was incensed because I consider it the most despicable act in the history of the game, but on the other side of the coin I was relieved that I now knew what I had always known in my heart, that we were a better baseball team on the field and with much more moral integrity.

Best regards,
Ralph Branca

BOBBY THOMSON *(pp. 84–87)*

Hi—

Going into last half of 9th inning losing 4 to 1, I felt totally depressed. I didn't think I would get a chance to hit, being the 5th hitter, with Newcombe looking so strong in the eight.

As it turned out, the score became 4 to 2 when I got up to bat. Don Mueller injuring his ankle sliding into third stopped the game for me—broke the tension—got my mind away from the game.

Wasn't until Mueller was carried off the field, my mind returned to the game. Walking to home plate, I was in my own world thinking about what I had to do: get back to fundamentals. Wait for the ball—don't get over anxious—do a good job—give yourself a chance to hit. I called myself an S.O.B. all the way to home plate. I had never done anything like that before in my life.

Arriving at home plate, I realized for the first time, the Dodgers had changed pitchers—I felt no pressure, just went through the motions, in my own little world, getting ready to hit.

I hit an inside fast ball for the homer and experienced excitement I hadn't felt before.

Sincerely,
Bobby Thomson

LAWRENCE GOLDBERG *(pp. 88–89)*

April 22, 2002

Dear Seth:

You asked how I came to record Russ Hodges' description of the Bobby Thomson home run—The Shot Heard Round the World.

I was 26 years old and working in an office in Manhattan. I knew I wouldn't have access to a radio but I wanted to hear the end of the playoff game. I was a long time Giant fan so I set the radio to WMCA, set up my reel to reel tape recorder, showed my Mother what button to push when the ninth inning started. I then took the BMT train to work.

That evening, I couldn't wait to get home to listen to the tape. I knew what had happened but I had to hear it for myself.

I rewound the tape and there was Russ Hodges screaming "The Giants win the pennant . . . I don't believe it . . . the whole place is going crazy."

The next day I wrote to Russ suggesting that if his station didn't record his "call" I could let him borrow my tape.

A few days later I got a call from Russ asking for the tape. I lent it to him. He used it to produce Christmas cards that year and returned the tape with a note of thanks.

The years have passed but everytime that home run is shown on TV—with the soundtrack based on my tape—I smile and think to myself: "We did that—Ralph Branca, Bobby Thomson, Russ Hodges, me and my MOTHER!"

Larry

PAUL LO DUCA *(pp. 90–91)*

Dear Seth,

My mother was such a big influence in my life. She taught me everything from patience and kindness to hardwork and determination. She was by my side and had a hand in all my accomplishments. From the soccer field, she would roam the sidelines to the baseball field, she cheered from the right field line. From the time she would take off work to sharpen my batting skills. Sometimes it was off to the batting cages but most of the time it took place right in out own back yard. With sunglasses to shield her eyes she threw me pinto bean after pinto bean 'til my hands bled. I can still feel her presence today. I can still hear her say "Keep your head down" on every bad swing. She will always be with me for as long as I live. The only thing I regret is that my mother never got to see me play at the Big League level. But one thing is for certain *Luci Lo Duca* and *the Lord* above both bleed "DODGER BLUE."

Paul Lo Duca

BARRY WILLIAMS *(pp. 92–95)*

March 23, 2002

Dear Seth,

Growing up in Los Angeles, I was naturally a Dodger fan. I recall how classes were stopped in my elementary school so we could gather in the auditorium to watch the historic 1963 World Series, which featured two amazing pitchers for the Dodgers—Don Drysdale and Sandy Koufax. As a little league pitcher (and a right hander) it was easy for me to relate to Drysdale. It was inspiring to watch as he dominated the batters, ultimately leading them on the victory in that series.

Nothing in my years was to prepare me for the day when the "The Big D" actually walked on to our Brady Bunch set. In addition to the anticipation of meeting him, the story line revolved around his teaching my character to play baseball and how to pitch. At 6'5" 220 pounds, he was someone to be reckoned with. I recall the rumors of his pitching days and his intimidating philosophy—"hit one of mine, I hit two of yours." I didn't know what to expect of the "real" person.

The man I met was open, friendly, commanding and helpful. He was on our set for two days and proved to be at ease in front of the camera as well. What impressed me most was what went on between takes. He

didn't retire to his dressing room or disappear from the sound stage. Instead he hung around with my Bradymates and me to . . . play catch. That was better than having a role on a series!

In life there are a few special, unforgettable experiences that are shaped by coming into contact with someone you truly admire. For me, the two days Don Drysdale came to our set to teach "Greg" how to pitch is one of them.

Kindly yours,
Barry Williams

BARRY ZITO *(pp. 96–97)*

(See typed letter.)

BARRY BREMEN *(pp. 98–99)*

9/10/2000

Seth,

I had just finished infield and outfield practice and all I was concerned about were the correct words to the national anthem. It was Tommy John who helped me into the stadium and the locker room. For a moment I was a New York Yankee! I will never forget how nervous I was.

When I joined the NBA All Stars, I wasn't sure what to expect. Would I be caught? Would I go to jail? What would happen? I was so nervous at first that I missed the basket all together and when I went for the rebound from George Gervin, well it had so much spin on it that I bobbled that also. I guess just nerves. My knees were weak and I was very light headed from all this excitement. The sounds of 80,000 fans were great! I had so much fun.

The moment I would never forget was when Otis Birdsong (who was a Kansas City King) and myself were talking on the sidelines and I had my Kansas City King uniform from four years before and he looked at me and said "You and I are on the same team and I don't even know who you is."

> My best to you always,
> Barry Bremen
> "The Impostor"

GENE MAUCH *(p. 100)*

A toothache hurts on either side of the mouth.
> Gene Mauch

MIKE VEECK *(pp. 101–103)*

11-27-2001
Dear Seth,

How do I view Disco Demolition 22 summers later? Through the years, people have said it was a disgrace; some said it was a tragedy. Some said I had it coming; my Dad, Bill Veeck said "sometimes they work too well." What did I learn? I never mistake a lousy promotion with a tragedy. Besides, I didn't have enough talent to be in "Rolling Stone" any other way.

> Fondly,
> Mike Veeck

JIMMY PIERSALL *(p. 104)*

(See typed letter.)

WILLIAM S. COHEN *(pp. 105–107)*

May 30, 2002
Dear Seth—

I played Little League at the tender age of 12. Except I was not very little. I stood 5'7" and weighed 125, considerably larger than most of my peers. I had a rocket arm with Nolan Ryan speed from the mound, which stood just 44 feet from home plate. However, I had all the control of an unguided Scud missile, and

serious injury was a very plausible outcome for those brave enough to step into the box.

This fear created by my lack of control was my greatest weapon. I earned the honor of pitching the first no-hitter in Maine Little League history. I also struck out 18 batters in one game while walking 16!

Given my control problems, very few batters dug their rubber spikes in & got close in the box. But opposing coaches used this against me. They would send tiny eight-year-olds to the plate who could barely hold the bat. Standing in a crouch, looking more bewildered than afraid, they were little more than two feet from head to toe. I was paralyzed with fear of hurting them and practically had to roll the ball to the plate. What I gave up in speed I did not gain in control. The Lilliputians humbled the Bangor Brobdingnagian as they walked to and around the bases with depressing regularity.

Through high school and college, I continued my pursuits on the mound, relishing the mano-a-mano challenge. I threw sliders, curve balls, & knucklers as off-speed pitches with great gusto, but with no greater control.

It was only after I entered politics that I learned to throw the perfect pitch—straight down the middle . . .

> Bill Cohen

TINKER TO EVERS TO CHANCE *(pp. 108–109)*

Johnny Evers letter:
June. 27. 34
Dear Mrs. Omberg:

Chance is dead ten years this coming month. Tinker lives in Orlando Florida.

I am glad I had the privalege of playing baseball with them.

> Sincerely,
> John Evers

Joe Tinker letter:

Oct 29th/45

Dear Mr. Smith

Chance is dead but you can write to Evers, Troy New York, although he is very sick. Best of luck and good health.

Sincerely,
Joe Tinker

RONALD REAGAN *(pp. 110–111)*

Oct. 1

Dear Friend—

Having met "Old Pete" you should be interested in knowing about, "the best kept secret in sports," which we hinted at in the picture. The "fainting spells" in our movie were as close to the truth as we felt we should go. In addition to all his other troubles or probably under lying all his troubles was the terrible affliction of "Epilepsy." He tried to keep this secret all his life and we felt we'd tell the story without using the word.

Best
Ronald Reagan

BOB WOLFF *(pp. 112–115)*

April 16, 2000

Dear Seth,

Opening Day in Washington was my best chance all season to shout at game's end, "The Senators are in first place!"

Not that the team lacked in talent—they lacked in numbers and in finances. They just couldn't afford enough stars at any one time.

It was exciting, competitive major league baseball though, and I was privileged to have a voice in it. When I arrived at Griffith Stadium for each new opener there was always hope— and there was preparation which included making a chart of who was in the presidential party and where each was sitting.

When Harry Truman was President, the big topic was whether he'd make his ceremonial pitch lefty or righty. The ambidextrous Chief Executive would not make this vital decision until the last moment.

President Eisenhower was passionate about golf, but a baseball fan too. Occasionally, unannounced, he left the White House early, along with his entourage, to watch a game. In 1956, with Ike in attendance, Jim Lemon put on a show with three home runs in one game. I always had the theory that if presidents had come out more often, the Senators would have won the pennant.

President Nixon knew the game and its players. One day, as Vice President, I interviewed him on radio as a "Fan in the Stands," and told him not to reveal his identity until the climactic moment. After seven minutes of baseball chatter, I inquired:

"And what do you do in Washington?"

"I work for the government."

"Well, that's just fine. We have so many government workers here. What's your job?"

"I'm the Vice-President of the United States!"

Good straight men are tough to find.

With best wishes, Seth,
Bob Wolff

SCOTT SHELDON *(p. 116)*

Dear Seth:

When I was a kid playing baseball, my dad said that when a coach/manager ever asked if I could play a position, I should say "sure." I never dreamed that it would ever happen.

When Johnny Oates asked if I wanted to do it that day I of course said "Sure, let's go for it." I felt most nervous though when I took the mound to face the only hitter of my professional career. I had to take a deep breath a couple of times and, incredibly, struck out the batter on a 67 MPH change-up.

What a joy it was to be able to do this on a

day when, without Johnny Oates's knowledge, my family, including my father, happened to be there in person to share this moment with me.

God Bless,
Scott Sheldon

JACK HAMILTON (p. 117)
(See typed letter.)

TIM SALMON (pp. 118–119)
Dear Seth,

Being a Major League dad offers many challenges and rewards. The season requires us to be on the road half the time. Mom ends up playing the role of dad much of the time. When the kids are young they seem to change a lot between road trips. I've missed out on a lot of "first time events." Some of the rewards are when the kids watch me on T.V. and being home most of the time during the off-season. My children are still young so I'm not sure if they can truly appreciate what I do. Their friends are my teammates' children and their dads are on T.V. also. So I'm not sure being on T.V. is a big deal. My hope is that I can play long enough so that when the kids are older they can come into the clubhouse and field and really enjoy it for what it's suppose to be . . . a dream come true!

Sincerely,
Tim

WAYNE CAUSEY (pp. 120–121)
Dear Seth,

The night Mr. Finley had the players ride the mules into the stadium—"Farmer's Night"—was only one of several mule events we had that year.

I most remember the mule event when the owner of the White Sox would not allow Mr. Finley to bring our team mascot, "Charlie O" The Mule, into Comisky Park. Because of this,

Finley hired several deliverymen to deliver a large carton to our dressing room during the game. When they opened the carton, inside, there was a donkey. They pushed & pulled the donkey through the tunnel, to the dugout & onto the field. The umpire told our manager to get the mule off the field or he would eject every player from the game. The mule was quite stubborn & the game was delayed for several minutes.

Wayne Causey

JACKIE BRANDT (p. 122)
Actually Seth,

I did have some shorts on. Most people watching on TV usually get to see everyone in uniform. I guess this was my chance to show them what a player looked like a home.

Jackie Brandt

FRANK THOMAS (p. 123)
April 14, 2001
Dear Seth:

Players like to eat and eat fast so on chartered flights, as soon as we were high enough, I would help the stewardesses serve the players. I served the players and manager first and the trainer got mad because I didn't serve him right away. He complained but it didn't do any good. He got over it.

I served on every road trip the whole season and the players liked it because they got their food a lot faster.

By the way, I always ate last.

Sincerely,
Frank Thomas
The Original One

SAMUEL GOLDWYN (pp. 124–126)
(See typed letter.)

ORLANDO CEPEDA *(p. 127)*

Seth—

My biggest moment in my career was my 1st big league game.

My 1st base hit was a homerun in my 1st game.

Watching Duke Snider, Pee Wee Reese and all those Dodger players in the same field with me was like a dream. The only thing that was missing was my father. He died three years before I play my 1st game in the big league.

> Orlando Cepeda
> HOF 99

THE AMAZING KRESKIN *(pp. 128–129)*

Feb. 26, 2001

Dear Seth,

My plan was to spend some time with the team in person to break what had become a mindset, what with the continuous losses. As it turned out I was only able to appear by phone on a radio show urging the fans to concentrate positively on their winning. I am told that cars pulled over to the sides of the roads during the time I set for a mass mental support. Had I gotten the team together at the same time, particularly if I saw them in person, I think I could have broken the slump by impressing on them a tremendous positive belief in their winning.

As for baseball in the year 2101 and to follow: I seriously believe it would be tragic if the sport were narrowed only to high paying ticketed audiences or to pay television. The American Sport, without any violence or greed, can give its fans a truly mystical experience.

> ESPecially,
> Kreskin

BOBBY BRAGAN *(pp. 130–131)*

(See typed letter.)

TODD ZEILE *(pp. 132–135)*

12-10-01

Dear Seth,

I recall being told at a very young age by my grandmother that she, and subsequently, I were direct descendants of two former United States Presidents: John Adams and John Quincy Adams.

I also recall thinking that it was "pretty cool," to be directly related to the Adam's Family (not to be confused with Gomez and Morticia) but nowhere as cool as my buddy whose grandfather animated the Flinstones' cartoon for Hanna Barberra. After all, could John Adams compare to having a grandfather who could whip out Fred Flinstone, George Jetson, or Scooby Doo in one fluid stroke of the pen?

This past year, that appreciation grew when I was fortunate enough to join a few of my teammates in our nation's capital. As I walked the halls of the West Wing and toured the inner sanctuary of our nation's government, I found myself more and more intrigued with the lives and impact of my presidential lineage. During the tour, we visited the original Senate Building, which now is a monument gallery.

On the floor of the Senate is a brass plaque with only the name "John Quincy Adams." Obviously intrigued, I asked our guide if he knew the genesis of the plaque. He said that during his tenure, Quincy always maintained his seat on that exact spot.

He then noted that Quincy was also notorious for resting his head on his desk and sleeping during Senate sessions. A bit disappointed, I asked if there was more to the story. With a smile, our guide asked me to stand on the plaque and face away from the majority of the room. He then explained to me that the Senate floor, as it is today, was split by Party affiliation, and that Quincy had the furthest desk from the opposing party.

Our guide then proceeded to walk to the opposite side of the Senate floor and whisper with his back to me. To my amazement, I could clearly understand every word. The marble floors and ceiling created a "whispering arch" which funneled directly to the spot in which Quincy's desk stood for years. He made a practice of eavesdropping on partisan issues and keeping a step ahead. Resourceful or deceitful? Either way, the Adam's Family legacy has proven to be one of the most innovative and influential in the history of our nation and thus has become a growing point of pride in my own family.

Sincerely,
Todd Zeile

DAVE MAY *(p. 136)*

Seth

When I heard I was traded for Hank Aaron, I was in a Chicago hotel, watching Wide World of Sports. At first I shocked. I left the meetings I have in Chicago for home in Milwaukee. The thing of being traded for Hank, just so he can finish his career there in Milwaukee, didn't rub too smooth with me. Because I wasn't just a throw in player. If I played right away when I got to Atlanta, I would've felt better about it. I had a manager who thought Hank was still there. I didn't play until they changed managers. I spent two long wasteless years in Atlanta. But now, when your career is long over and your part of a question, it's a part of your baseball career you can add to your stats.

Dave

JOEL YOUNGBLOOD *(pp. 137–139)*

Seth,

So it's Saturday morning . . . we started the game at 1:05. I was with the Mets and we were playing the Cubs. It was the 4th inning at Wrigley Field, and Joe Torre, my manager, called me over when we were in the dugout and told me that he was taking me out of the game.

I said, "Joe, why are you taking me out of the game? I already have a double and knocked in a couple of runs" (which turned out to be the game-winning runs—off Hall of Famer Ferguson Jenkins, no less!) Torre told me, the reason he was pulling me was because I had just literally been traded by the Mets to the Montreal Expos. He had to take me out because I wasn't a Met anymore.

Montreal was short of players so they asked if the Mets could send me immediately (the Expos were playing in Philadelphia).

What happened next was a total whirlwind: I quickly said goodby to my teammates in the clubhouse, took off my uniform; took a shower, packed my baseball equipment, got in a cab; went to my hotel, packed my clothes, checked out of the hotel, made reservations to fly to Philadelphia and got back in the cab and headed for the airport. As I got into the taxicab, ready to take me to O'Hare, I realized I made a terrible mistake: I left my glove on the dugout steps at Wrigley Field.

I had packed everything but my glove. My glove at that time was more important than the flight. Because I had used this glove for, like, 14 years. So, back to Wrigley, where I ran inside, picked my glove up, told my now ex-teammates "bye" again, ran outside, got in the cab and sprinted to the plane to Philly, barely making it.

When I landed in Philly, I called a cab, waited for my bags, just like a regular tourist, and went to Veterans Stadium, where it was the eighth inning of the game there between the Phillies and my new team the Montreal Expos. This all happened so fast!

I went inside the clubhouse, put my new uniform on, walked into the Expos dugout. And before I knew it, I was called into the game as a pitch hitter. This time I would be facing another great Hall-of-Famer to be, Steve Carlton. And wouldn't you know, I got a base hit off "Lefty" too. The next day I woke up and an article in the paper said that I was the only player in Major League Baseball history to have two hits playing for two different teams in two different cities in one day.

And I'm pretty sure I used the same baseball bat for both hits!

All the best Seth,

Joel Youngblood

RANDY VELARDE (p. 140)
Dear Seth,

I was very upset before "the play" occurred. Because I had just "booted" a routine double-play ball. So if you believe in fate, the triple play would not have occurred if I hadn't made this error.

Omar Olivares works Shane Spencer to a full count. As he (Omar) delivers his 3-2 pitch I notice the runners, (Jorge Posada on first & Tino Martinez on second) moving on the pitch. Just then, Shane hits a soft line drive to right where I was playing him, shade up the middle. I catch it, tag second, then Jorge. History! Routine triple-play! If there's such a thing. Ha.

Being a veteran on this team has definitely tested my patience level. But its worked good for both parties. Instead of me being so introverted, I'm opening up to these kids. With 13 plus yrs. of experience at the major league level I've seen a lot. So I take it upon myself to help anyway possible. Such as defensive set

ups, opposing pitchers tendencies and yes, umpires. What zone's each has.

I'm not big on <u>vocal</u> leadership. To me, action carries more weight. But if I'm hard pressed, HEADS WILL TURN!

Sincerely,

Randy Velarde

FLOYD BAKER (p. 141)
4/11/2000
Dear Mr. Swirsky,

Dizzy was throwing every off speed type pitch, you could think of, in other words a lot of <u>junk</u>— not enough to hit but enough to fool. I didn't get a hit off him.

We were all having a good time and enjoying every minute of it. No player ever thought Dizzy was trying to show them up; it was a thrill to bat against him.

There will never be another Dizzy Dean.

Sincerely,

Floyd Baker

LESLIE WAGNER BLAIR (pp. 142–145)
Dear Seth,

Today when a person hears the words, Honus Wagner, most think of the world famous baseball trading card. My grandfather would be embarrassed with all the hype placed on a piece of paper bearing his likeness. The reason he had the cards pulled from the T206 baseball card set was that he loved children and he did not want them to have to buy tobacco in order to have his cards. I was excited to see for what the card finally sold. And, NO, I do not have one. I wish I had!

In his spare him, Buck loved to fish. I remember my mother, Betty telling me Dwight Eisenhower wanted to meet with Buck. But, Buck was going fishing that day. It wasn't that he didn't want to see Ike, but it was Buck's day to fish! So, Ike's entire entourage went out to the "watering hole" and for a while those two talked and fished!

Even decades after my grandfather retired to the great "diamond in the sky," I still remember him fondly. When people ask me what I got from him, I can truly say, love and memories, but <u>NOT</u> his bow legs!

Leslie Wagner Blair

GOOSE GOSSAGE (p. 146)

Seth,

I did see Nettles catch many pop-ups throughout our times together. But I had never really watched that closely where he caught the ball. On this particular pop-up, I watched every second of it.

When it finally reached Nettles' glove, I was watching for the catch to be made with arms extended, but instead, his glove was next to his shoulder.

For a split second my heart kinda' stopped, for I thought he had missed it. Whew!

"Goose"

HUGH MULCAHY (p. 147)

July 4, 2000
Hi Seth,

Got along very well with the fellows in my outfit and some of them seemed interested in the "ups and downs" of a baseball player.

Didn't think too much about baseball. My thoughts were mostly on my family at home.

As far as the army life I was very fortunate. When I was in New Guinea and the Phillipines the fighting was 50 to 75 miles north of my outfit. After being in each area for four or five months we played several ball games.

Best wishes,
Sincerely
Hugh Mulcahy

MARGARET JOY (pp. 148–151)

2-10-2001
Dear Seth,

About my brother, Ray; I could write reams about him. Besides being an athlete, he was real "arty." He was very musical—could sing beautifully and whistle like a charm. The neighbors always said they knew when he was home because they could hear him whistling. He was so high-spirited and such a joy to be around. He just lit up the place!

When in New York, he would attend all his good friend Al Jolson's performances; also the Follies.

After a ballgame in St. Louis, there was a little boy selling newspapers at the train. Ray said, "Whose boy are you Cal," and the boy replied, "Chappy's boy!" Then Ray threw him some money. That was typical of my brother. He was so personable and so caring.

As to his untimely death, it was a tragedy for our family. My family did not get the message that Ray had been hurt. Only a telegram that he was dead. My mother collapsed and had to have Doctor care. We were devastated! He had been so wonderful to my parents and my brother and me.

Just a word about the funeral service—It was in the Cathedral downtown. Such a crowd. They had to make way for us to get into the church—men tipped their hats as the casket was carried into the building. The choir sang a lovely rendition of Lord Kindly Light. Strange that I would remember that.

Seth, that's my story as I remember it. I appreciate the fact that you are interested in my brother. He was a true gentleman and you would have loved knowing him. God bless.

Margaret (Chapman) Joy

WALTER CRONKITE *(p. 152)*
(See typed letter.)

GABE KAPLER *(p. 153)*
Dear Seth,

The first major league game I went to was at Chavez Ravine to see the Dodgers. I will surely remember the first game I take my son Chase to see. I will be playing in it!

I enjoy watching games very much because I can relax and enjoy it. That is my biggest challenge today—enjoying the time I spend in baseball. Sometimes I get so caught up in performing and having success that I forget to enjoy myself.

My #1 quote about baseball—describes it to a 'T' for me: "Baseball can bring me the ultimate pleasure—It can also cause me the ultimate pain." In a word, sweet-n-sour. I just made it one word.

Sincerely,
Gabriel Kapler

BILL FREEHAN *(pp. 154–155)*
Seth:

Doug Harvey took his time to see if I held on to the ball—as Lou tried to run me over instead of sliding. If you look at the films you will see him come back and try to "re-touch" home plate—I then re-touched him.

He maintains that—why should I touch him a 2nd time if I had done it the first time. My response was: why were you coming back to touch it again if you touched it the 1st time.

However all the above is moot! Check the "Box Scores" and that is the only real criteria— "the ump said out!" How many historical sports events have been decided on snap decisions by officials.

I have looked at the photo's and replays a million times and no one can tell conclusively what happened.

The result—It was close! The ump called him out! The series took a turn and I've got a 1968 World Series Ring that says "1968 World Champions".

By the way—Lou Brock is a great guy—a good friend and we have re-enacted this play numerous times at "Old-Timers Games."

My Best!
Bill Freehan

ERNIE HARWELL *(pp. 156–157)*
March 9, 2000
Dear Seth:

Because I was a song writer, Tiger GM Jim Campbell appointed me to select anthem singers for '68 World Series. For first two games in Detroit I picked Margaret Whiting and Marvin Gaye.

A friend in record business told me that José Feliciano had thrilled the Greek Theater audience in Hollywood with his rendition of the anthem.

José agreed to come & sing for the 5th game. His performance caused an uproar. The NY Times printed his photo on page one as he strummed his guitar and sang in center field.

It was a watermark in anthem singing. He rendered a soulful, haunting version.

I think the uproar came because
1) It was different
2) José was singing in midst of troubled times and because of the guitar was identified with the "hippie" movement.
3) Many fans felt he had long hair—another hippy characteristic.

I almost lost my job because of the uproar. But I stood up for José and took blame for the selection.

Best wishes—
Ernie Harwell

STEVE SWIRSKY *(pp. 158–159)*

August 11, 2001

Dear Seth:

You used to love to hear this story when you were growing up. In the mid-1950's, after years in Little League, I played in the Babe Ruth League. At 13, I was selected for the All-Star team to compete for the Conn. state championship with my melting-pot team: Italian and Irish kids from "the hill" section of New Haven, black kids from the Dixwell Ave section and Jews from Westville, the small suburb where I lived.

We all thought we'd be the next Joe DiMaggio or Willie Mays and winning the state title definitly fueled that fantasy. We went on to the New England championship in Cranston, R.I., winning the first two games in the round-robin single-loss elimination. In the final game we were trailing 7-2, with 2 out in the bottom of the last inning. Things looked so bleak that I took off my spikes and resigned myself to the long bus ride home.

My coach told me to put them back on. "We still have a shot!" he said. What followed was a baseball miracle: two walks, an error, a double, a hit batter and two singles. The game was now 7-6 with two outs and my turn at bat. Our opponents had simply run out of gas—and heart! In an entire lifetime, a few days stand out—this was one of mine.

With bases loaded, I drilled the first pitch into right-centerfield to win the game 8-7. Revved from our come from behind victory, our team took a cross-country train to the Babe Ruth World Series in Portland, Oregon—full of optimism and a burning desire to win.

It wasn't long before reality set back in. The first pitcher we faced was future legend Mickey Lolich, only 15 at the time but, even then clearly destined for the Majors.

I was the clean-up hitter and he struck me out three times with only ten pitches. We lost 8-0. I didn't do much better against future Yankee star Al Downing. The message was unmistakable: You're good – but not that good! That dose of reality was an important lesson for those of us not fated to be in the "bigs."

Baseball is a great teacher of sportsmanship, endurance, focus, patience, respect for teammates and coaches and what the essence of <u>fun</u> is all about.

Love,
Dad

NAT FEIN *(pp. 160–161)*

8-28-99

Dear Seth,

It was a gloomy day at Yankee Stadium. Babe Ruth was making his final appearance after years of playing baseball. Thousands of fans had jammed the stadium to say goodbye to Ruth.

The Babe came out of the dugout, waving and walked slowly to homeplate. The band began to play "Auld Lang Syne." It was a tremendous emotional experience. George Herman Ruth stepped forward. No one could mistake that figure. His wide shoulders slightly stooped as he leaned on his baseball bat to steady himself. The crowd rose in tribute to the man who was the idol of millions.

Twenty-five photographers were there covering the Babe. None of the photos I made told the story. The fact that Babe Ruth's number 3 would never be used again had to be included so I left the other photographers and walked around Ruth. Then I saw it—The <u>composition</u> that told the story in one picture, the "Babe Bows Out." Luck was with me.

Nat Fein

Bibliography

The Baseball Encyclopedia, 10th ed. New York: Macmillan, 1996.

The Editors of *The Sporting News: Baseball.* New York: Galahad Books, 1993.

Dewey, Donald, and Nicholas Acocella. *The Biographical History of Baseball.* New York: Galahad Books, 1993.

Koppett, Leonard. *Koppett's Concise History of Major League Baseball.* Philadelphia: Temple University Press, 1998.

Light, Jonathon Fraser. *The Cultural Encyclopedia of Baseball.* Jefferson, N.C.: McFarland & Company, 1997.

Photography Credits

Peering through fence (p. ii); Bob Wolff (p. 112); Lou Gehrig and Joe DiMaggio photos (p. 126); Grover Cleveland Alexander (p. 111); Jimmy Piersall (p. 104); Buck O'Neil (p. 51); Hugh Mulcahy (p. 147); Ray Chapman (p. 148); Goose Gossage (p. 146); The Dodgers Sym-phony (p. 78); Tinker to Evers to Chance photos (pp. 108–109); Ernie Harwell (p. 156)—National Baseball Library and Archive, Cooperstown, New York. Thank you, W. C. Burdick.

Richie Scheinblum (p. 50); Gene Mauch (p. 100); Randy Velarde (p. 140); Gates Brown (p. 12); Dave May (p. 136); Frank Pytlack (p. 58); Joel Youngblood photos (p. 137); Jim Campanis photos (p. 59); Gaylord Perry (p. 33); Jackie Brandt (p. 122); Ralph Branca (p. 80); Orlando Cepeda (p. 127); Jack Hamilton (p. 117)—George Brace Photo. Thanks, Mary and George.

Disco Demolition Night (pp. 102–103); Babe Ruth playing bass drum, saxophone, tuba, and piano (p. 15); Babe Ruth with family around piano (p. 14); old men listening to game (p. 87); people watching Thomson game in S.F. (p. 84); Bobby Thomson (p. 85); Thomson celebrating with Jansen and Maglie (p. 86); Russ Hodges's microphone (p. 89); Tony Conigliaro (p. 117); Don Drysdale (p. 95); Jackie Robinson (p. 53); George Bush and Babe Ruth (p. 2); George W. Bush throwing out first pitch (p. 46); Mo Vaughn (p. 52); newsboy (p. 149); Bud Selig (p. 54); Samuel Goldwyn (p. 125); Ernie Banks (p. 30)—UPI/Corbis-Bettmann Archives. Thank you, Katie Shanks.

President George W. Bush and father, #43 and #41 (p. 48); Tony Saunders (p. 60); Paul McCartney and Heather Mills (p. 16); Charlie Finley (p. 121); Mel Allen (p. 152); Walter Cronkite (p. 152)—AP/Wide World Photo.

Bert Campaneris (p. 116); Wayne Causey (p. 120); Babe Ruth (p. 72); Dizzy Dean (p. 141)—*The Sporting News.* Thanks to Steve Gietschier.

John Adams (p. 133)—Harvard University Portrait Collection.

John Quincy Adams (p. 134)—Meserve Kunhardt Collection.

Richard Nixon (p. 115)—*Washington Post,* courtesy of the D.C. Public Library.

Dwight Eisenhower (p. 114); Harry Frazee (p. 70)—*U.S. News* Collection, Library of Congress.

Harry Truman (p. 113)—Harry S. Truman Library.

The Monkees (p. 36); *The Brady Bunch* (p. 92); Elliott Gould (p. 22)—michaelochsarchives.com.

Max Frazee (p. 71)—Marty Appel.

Ken Keltner (p. 58)—Cleveland Public Library.

"Fans Protest Soul Singer's Anthem Version" article (p. 157); "U.S. Attacked" headline (p. 55)—the *New York Times.*

Bobby Bragan (p. 130)—Neils Lauritzen, *The Milwaukee Journal,* © 2001 Journal Sentinel Inc., reproduced with permission.

George W. Bush in Little League uniform, and as an infant sitting on father's shoulders (p. 48)—George Bush Presidential Library.

George Bush tossing ball (p. 49)—David Valdez, the White House.

"Seaver Perfect Till 9th . . ." newspaper (p. 26); black cat (pp. 28–29); "brothers in arms" (p. 190)—the *Daily News.*

José Feliciano (p. 157)—*Detroit Free Press.*

Peter Ueberroth and Jean Yawkey (p. 64)—the *Boston Globe.*

Flip Schulke (p. 4)—Gary Truman.

Martin Luther King and family (pp. 6–8)—© Flip Schulke.

Ronald Reagan in *The Winning Team* (p. 110)—© 1952 Warner Bros. All Rights Reserved.

Shane Halter (p. 116)—courtesy of the Detroit Tigers (thank you, Melanie Halter).

Paul Lo Duca (p. 90); Shawn Green (pp. 17, 19)—courtesy of the Los Angeles Dodgers (thank you, Charise Weller).

Bob Costas (p. 62) (thank you, Pam Davis); Tim Russert (p. 42)—courtesy of NBC News.

Russert family (p. 44)—courtesy of Tim Russert (thank you, Lisa Havlovitz).

William S. Cohen (pp. 105, 107)—courtesy of William S. Cohen.

Tim Salmon family (p. 118)—courtesy of the Anaheim Angels.

Mookie Wilson (p. 66); Todd Zeile (p. 132)—courtesy of the New York Mets.

Elliott Gould and Donny Kramer (p. 24)—courtesy of Elliott Gould.

Graig Nettles photos (p. 146); Ron Swoboda (p. 35)—courtesy of Stone Henry.

Buzz Aldrin (p. 34)—courtesy of Buzz Aldrin.

Bill Freehan (p. 154)—Richard Bak.

Honus Wagner (pp. 142, 144)—courtesy of Leslie Wagner Blair (family photos) and Stone Henry (baseball card).

Barry Williams and Don Drysdale (p. 94)—courtesy of Viacom Consumer Products, Barry Williams, and Ann Meyers-Drysdale. (Thank you, Nick Lampros, Anthony Anzaldo, Paul Hrisko, and Donna Carter.)

Scott Sheldon (p. 116); Gabe Kapler (p. 153)—courtesy of the Texas Rangers.

Edward M. Kennedy (p. 10)—courtesy of Senator Kennedy.

Aurelio Rodriguez baseball card (p. 20)—courtesy of Topps, Inc.

Elizabeth Wrigley-Field (p. 32)—courtesy of of Elizabeth Wrigley-Field.

Peter Tork (p. 38)—courtesy of Bonnie Verrico.

Ed Rendell and Michael Springer (p. 56)—courtesy of Walt Matweychuk.

"The Babe Bows Out" (p. 160)—courtesy of Nat Fein.

Paul Giorgio photos (p. 68)—courtesy of Paul Giorgio.

The Amazing Kreskin (p. 128)—courtesy of the Amazing Kreskin.

Eddie Layton (p. 77); Bob Sheppard (p. 76)—courtesy of Paul Doherty.

Bob Mallon (p. 74)—courtesy of Bob Mallon.

Lawrence Goldberg (p. 88)—courtesy of Leonard Goldberg.

Barry Zito (pp. 96–97)—courtesy of Barry Zito.

White House (p. 47)—courtesy of Meserve Kunhardt Collection (top) and Library of Congress (bottom).

Red Sox wine bottle (p. 65); Terminal Tower ball (p. 58); "the Mookie ball" (p. 66); Tom Seaver's jersey (p. 27); Dizzy Dean's last glove (p. 141); 1969 Topps baseball card box (p. 21); Joe DiMaggio press statement (p. 126); Babe Ruth letter (p. 73); Walter Cronkite letter (p. 152); Bob Mallon letter (p. 75); Samuel Goldwyn letter (pp. 124–125); Ronald Reagan letter (p. 111); Tinker and Evers letters (p. 109); Ray Chapman's funeral photo (p. 150); Cornelius Savage photo (p. 40); photo of Lou Gehrig and his mother (p. 124); photo of Barry Bremer (p. 98); Cesar Tovar (p. 116); photo of Steve Swirsky (p. 158); Ebbets Field photo (p. 79)—from the collection of the author.

Production and Typesetting by erictolladay@pixelectomy.com

Acknowledgments

First, to the people who wrote the letters that appear in this book, thank you for sharing your personal thoughts and memories.

To my editor at Crown, Pete Fornatale, who steadfastly believed in this project from day one. Many thanks to Steve Ross, Annik LaFarge, and Dorianne Steele, along with the entire dedicated staff at Crown.

To Elena Nachmanoff, a thousand thank yous wouldn't begin to express my gratitude to you for your help on this project. I treasure our friendship.

I want to express my deepest and most heartfelt thanks to a wonderful, sweet woman named Darci Ross. Darci passed away toward the end of this project. She was a true friend who consistently helped me with all my books. Her warm spirit lies within this book's pages. Thank you, Darc, for your style and your smile.

To Matt Bialer, my literary agent, thank you for your ongoing and never-wavering support and friendship.

And thank you to the following people for taking time out of their very busy lives for their assistance on this project: Marlene Adler; Marty Adler; Terry Anzaldo; Lani Arst; Pam Backer; Jeff Balash; A. Scott Berg; Jack Berke; John Branca; Don Cromwell; Paul Doherty; Joanne Drake; John Eastman; Morris Engelberg; Erin Estrada; Herb Fagen; Kevin Feeley; Tom Frechette; Samuel Goldwyn, Jr.; Suzanne Gannon; Victoria Grasso; Gary Green; Amy Guenter; Phyllis Halpern; Bill Henry; Jay Horwitz; David Howard (a special thank you!); Karen Hughes; Jennifer Kan; Ken Khachigian; Andrew Lack; Aimee Leone; Nancy Mazmanian; Kevin McCormick; Tim Mead; Melody Miller; Carmen Molina; John Olguin; Helene Petillo; Nancy Reagan; Paul Reiferson; Scott Ross; Rick Solomon; my totally amazing mother, Joan Swirsky; Arn Tellem; Bob Tyrer; Keith Vari; Scott Vecera; Bonnie Verrico; Robert Vickers; Diane Walsh; Mary Jane Wick; Joel Wolfe; Jim Young.

I also want to acknowledge the late Dick Schaap, one of those people you meet and you feel lucky that you did— a great man.

To Julian and Luke, I'm so honored to be your dad.

And to the love of my life, my wife, Jody. Thank you for always believing in all my creative endeavors.

Much love.

About the Author

Seth Swirsky is a songwriter with EMI Music Publishing who has written hits for numerous recording artists, among them Taylor Dayne ("Tell It to My Heart"), Al Green, Tina Turner, and Rufus Wainwright. His CD will be released in May, 2003. *Something to Write Home About* follows his best-sellers *Baseball Letters* (1996) and *Every Pitcher Tells a Story* (1999). A Dartmouth graduate, the author is a noted collector of baseball memorabilia; his collection can be viewed at Seth.com. He lives in Los Angeles with his wife, Jody Gerson, and their sons, Julian and Luke.

Brothers in arms: Kian and Milad Momeni (ages 3 and 6) before game one of the Yankees-Mets Subway Series in 2000.

...ing their rubber spikes in a ... close ...
But opposing coaches used this against ...
would send tiny eight-year-olds to the ...
who could barely hold the bat. Stan...
...rouch, looking more bewildered than ...
they were little more than two feet f...
to toe. I was paralyzed with fear of h...
and practically had to roll the ball...
plate. What I gave up in speed I ...
in control. The Lilliputians humbled th...
Brobdingnagian* as they walked to and ...
the bases with depressing regularity.

Through high school and college,

...on rubber spikes in a hot ... in the box...

...posing coaches used this against me. T...

...send tiny eight-year-olds to the pl...

...ould barely hold the bat. Standing...

..., looking more bewildered than a fr...

...are little more than two feet from h...

...I was paralyzed with fear of hurting...

...actually had to roll the ball to...

...what I gave up in speed I did not...

...trol. The Lilliputians humbled the Ba...

...regian* as they walked to and from...

...ses with depressing regularity.

...rough high school and college, I cont...